Michael Tintner is a freelance writer, specialising in financial advertising. He was educated at Cambridge, then worked as a copywriter for several leading advertising agencies.

Michael Tintner has written two other books: *Marketing Your Business* and *Atlas of Knowledge*.

# STATE IMPERFECT

## THE BOOK OF
## SOCIAL PROBLEMS

## MICHAEL TINTNER

An Optima book

© Michael Tintner, 1989

First published in 1989 by
Macdonald Optima, a division of
Macdonald & Co. (Publishers) Ltd
66–73 Shoe Lane
London EC4P 4AB

A member of Maxwell Pergamon Publishing Corporation plc

British Library Cataloguing in Publication Data

Tintner, Michael
    State imperfect: the book
    1. Great Britain. Social problems
    I. Title
    361.1′0941

    ISBN 0-356-17981-8

Photoset in Great Britain by Leaper & Gard

Printed and bound in Great Britain by
Richard Clay Ltd, Bungay, Suffolk

# CONTENTS

## Part One: Health

### Deaths

### Disability

### Diseases

# CONTENTS

# CONTENTS

# CONTENTS

# THE UNITED KINGDOM
# VITAL STATISTICS

## POPULATION

| | |
|---|---|
| Total: | 56.9 million |
| Males | 27.7 million |
| Females | 29.2 million |
| England | 47.7 million |
| Northern Ireland | 1.6 million |
| Scotland | 5.1 million |
| Wales | 2.8 million |
| Children (under 15) | 10.8 million |
| Over the age of 59 | 11.8 million |

## LAND AREA

| | sq miles | sq km |
|---|---|---|
| | 94,475 | 244,755 |
| England | 50,320 | 130,360 |
| Northern Ireland | 5,460 | 14,150 |
| Scotland | 30,400 | 78,750 |
| Wales | 8,015 | 20,760 |

# INTRODUCTION

## Why an Atlas of Social Problems?

Until now, no book, or source of information, has presented the vital statistics on the social problems of the United Kingdom in a simple, accessible format. There are various government publications, particularly *Social Trends*, which provide many of the relevant figures, but most are neither simple nor accessible (as well as being expensive) — and none focusses exclusively on social problems. No one, it seems, wants to be the bearer of bad news alone.

The result is that most people have only a sketchy idea of how bad (or good) things are in the United Kingdom. They may know a few statistics like the numbers of unemployed, but will have little idea about how many people are living in poverty, or alcoholic, or disabled; or the extent of criminal activity; or details of the pollution of the environment.

## Problems Looking For Solutions

*State Imperfect* aims to be objective and balanced, although inevitably it springs from a 'liberal' outlook. The issues covered here qualify as social problems in differing degrees; indeed some may not be seen as problems at all. *State Imperfect* has followed a wide brief in selecting problems on the grounds that it is better to have the information than not.

Neither does *State Imperfect* take a particular political stance. The government comes in for some criticism, as any government would, though the first concern is not to lay blame, but to present *problems-to-be-solved*, problems for which there are often no readymade, satisfactory solutions on the left, right or centre of the political spectrum; many, such as currently incurable diseases, absolutely demand new, creative solutions.

## How To Use This Book: Interpreting Statistics

All statistics must be treated with caution, if not downright scepticism. Some are estimates of national totals based on small or very small samples; some are only rough stabs by a concerned charity; none can convey the quality as opposed to the quantity of a particular problem. But most at least give a rough idea of a given situation, and many are remarkably consistent over the years. It is fascinating, for example, how little certain statistics like the numbers of suicides, or deaths on the road, change year in, year out — although, long-term, they may be moving slowly upwards or downwards.

Other points to bear in mind when comparing and interpreting statistics, are:

**Country.**    Not all 'national' statistics are based on the same 'nation'; some are based just on England, some on England and Wales, some on England, Wales and Scotland (i.e. Great Britain), yet others on Northern Ireland as well (i.e. the United Kingdom). This can be unavoidable because, for example, England and Wales have a different legal system to Scotland.

**Date.**    Another major difficulty is the dates of different statistics. The latest available figures on any problem can, depending on the problem, refer to anything from last month, to up to four years, and occasionally, even further back. In addition, figures can refer to different time periods — from January to December, or from April to April. It is still impossible to take a single comprehensive statistical snapshot of the United Kingdom at any point in time.

**Class.**    Different sources use different definitions of socio-economic groups, and are referred to accordingly. The Institute of Practitioners in Advertising definition goes from A (higher management) to E (pensioners, casual workers or long-term unemployed); the OPCS (Office of Population Censuses and Surveys) scale goes from I (professional) to V (unskilled).

**Rounding Up.** Many figures are rounded up to the nearest thousand or hundred or whole. Neat figures therefore have often been rounded up and component statistics may not add up to a given total.

**Sources.** On many problems *State Imperfect* has used a variety of sources. The main one(s) are listed at the end of each section in capitals (SOURCE: ——); those for isolated statistics are listed under sub-sections (Source: ——).

**Further Reading and Useful Addresses.** If you want to find out more about a particular problem, the main statistical sources and bodies are listed at the end of the book.

## What Would It Cost To Abolish Poverty?

Poverty is perhaps the most fundamental social problem, one in which so many other problems such as poor housing and poor health are rooted. Alan Walker, Professor of Social Policy at the University of Sheffield, has been researching and writing on social problems and social policy for twenty years. He has been invited to calculate the cost of abolishing poverty.

You may disagree with his *approach* to abolishing poverty, which depends on the use of state benefits. But it does put a minimum figure for the first time on the *cost* of abolishing poverty. Thus it sets a target at which people of whatever political persuasion can aim — and that target, as it turns out, is not beyond our wildest dreams.

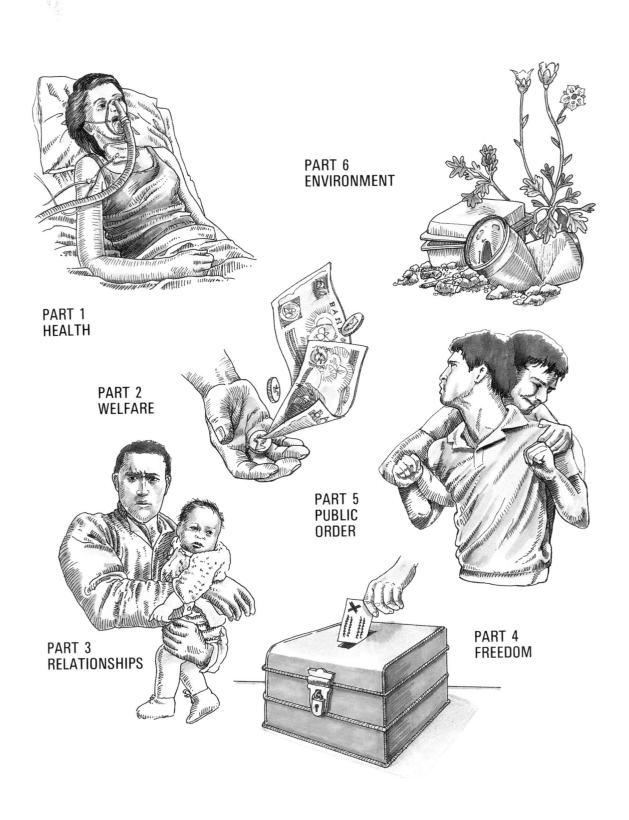

PART 6
ENVIRONMENT

PART 1
HEALTH

PART 2
WELFARE

PART 5
PUBLIC
ORDER

PART 3
RELATIONSHIPS

PART 4
FREEDOM

# SOCIAL PROBLEMS

The main areas of social problems are the main areas of a human being's life — health, welfare, relationships, freedom, public order, and environment. Social problems occur, for the most part, when there is a serious impoverishment of any of these areas affecting the lives of large groups of people.

Different areas can often be inter-related — people in poverty may well have health problems, live in unhealthy environments, and lack basic freedoms. But areas may also be entirely separate — a person who is disabled may be rich in all other areas of life.

There is no definitive way of categorising social problems. The underlying approach here has been to look at social problems from the viewpoint of the individual and the individual's life.

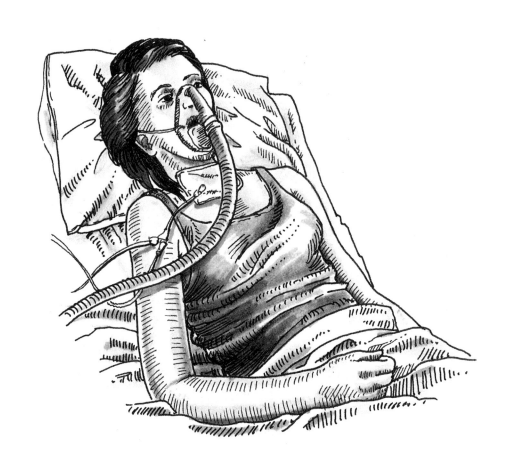

# PART ONE
# HEALTH

The problems of health, or ill-health, come first in the book because they can be the most difficult to solve. Poverty can in principle be cured, many disabilities and diseases cannot. They present medical as well as economic challenges.

Fatal diseases (under Deaths) are dealt with separately from non-fatal diseases (under Disease). Some diseases fall into both categories but the distinction nevertheless seems worth making.

The health record of the United Kingdom is grim compared to that of many other developed countries, and we have been called 'the sick man of Europe'. We have far too many premature deaths, one of the world's highest rates of deaths from heart diseases, and around 100,000 deaths every year which are smoking-related. The United Kingdom has one of the world's best records for road accidents, but we still lose far too many people through drink-driving. And there are millions of disabled, whose special needs are often too easily overlooked.

# PREMATURE DEATHS

## 138,931
**premature deaths (UK, 1986)**

**Cemetery, Southport**

Although people are, on average, living longer and longer as the century progresses, there are still a great many 'premature deaths', i.e. deaths before 65. Most result not from accidents or violence, but from 'diseases of civilization', such as heart disease and lung cancer, which could be prevented.

## Total deaths and births in the United Kingdom in 1986

Deaths    660,735 (11.6 per 1,000 population)
Births    727,000 (13.2 per 1,000 population)

# PREMATURE DEATHS

## How?

Mainly people die of diseases. Accidents and violence account for only a tiny percentage of all deaths.

| | |
|---|---|
| Natural Causes | 638,346 deaths (97%) |
| Accidents and Violence | 22,389 deaths (3%) |

## Who?

**M/F.** Men are much more likely to die prematurely than women. 86,989 men died prematurely compared with 51,942 women. But the overall death rate for men at 11.8 per 1,000 population is only slightly higher than the 11.5 rate for women. Overall, 327,160 males died in 1986, and 333,575 females.

More men die as a result of accidents or violence — 4.1% in 1987, against 2.5% for women.

**Age.** 58% of people dying prematurely were aged 55-65 (50,352 men and 29,954 women). Another 19% were aged 45-54. 11% of premature deaths occurred under the age of 25 — almost half of these in the first year of life.

**Class.** The poorer classes are much more likely to die young than the richer classes. **Unskilled workers, in particular, run at least twice the annual risk of death as professionals.** The Standard Mortality Ratio (SMR) for unskilled men in England and Wales is 131, compared to 63 for professional men, and 100 for the population as a whole. Deaths among children under the age of 15 steadily increase as you move further down the socio-economic scale.

Sources: Social Trends 1988; Occupational Mortality, Childhood Supplement, OPCS 1988.

## Occupations.

Some jobs are much more stressful and/or dangerous than others, as this table for men aged 20-64 in Great Britain shows. Generally, professional and white collar workers have a lower mortality than manual workers.

| Occupation | Mortality ratio |
|---|---|
| Scaffolders | 151% |
| Oil rig workers | 147% |
| Members of the armed forces | 145% |
| Factory workers | 132% |
| Builders | 107% |
| Miners | 104% |
| Police | 94% |
| Journalists | 87% |
| Members of the legal profession | 74% |
| Farmers | 72% |
| Civil servants | 72% |
| Clergymen | 70% |
| Doctors | 65% |
| Scientists | 60% |
| Dentists | 59% |
| Financial managers | 43% |

Source: Occupational Mortality, 1979-80, 1982-3, decennial supplement, OPCS 1986.

## Regions

As a general rule, mortality rates are higher outside London and the South East (with a death rate of 10.9 per 1,000 population in 1986). The North West has the highest rate in the country at 12.5. Two notable exceptions are the South West with a death rate of 12.4 (perhaps because it has more retired people) and Northern Ireland which has the lowest death rate in the UK at 10.3.

Source: Regional Trends 1988.

## Trends

The death rate has fluctuated but not altered much since 1971 when it was very slightly lower at 11.5 per 1,000.

SOURCE: Annual Abstract of Statistics 1988.

# LIFE EXPECTANCY

## 71 for boys
## born in the UK, 1985
## 77 for girls
## born in the UK, 1985

Life expectancy is now much higher than it was at the beginning of the century, when boys could only expect to live to the age of 48 and girls to 52. Nevertheless the elderly can expect a shorter life in Britain than many other places. One consequence of higher life expectancy is the proportional growth of the elderly, who at nearly 10 million in Britain, are approaching a fifth of the population, and whose special needs will require more attention.

There is still much to be explained about why women live so much longer, not only in the United Kingdom, but in almost every developed country. Although it's a well-known fact, comparatively little systematic research has been done on the causes.

## Who?

**M/F.** Two-thirds of the pensionable population are women, with almost TWO women for every man, among the 75-84's, and THREE to one for the over 85's.

Source: Social Trends 1989, Help the Aged.

**Over 100.** Over 3 in 1,000 infants born today can be expected to live longer than 100.

Source: Social Trends 1988.

## International comparison

In 21 other countries, including Sri Lanka and Uruguay, a 65-year-old man can expect to live longer than in the UK. Women of the same age will live longer in 16 other countries, including Portugal, Greece, and Spain. A 1988 Age Concern report argues that severe poverty among our elderly is partly to blame.

Source: World Health Organisation 1988.

## Trends

Life expectancy has been improving steadily throughout the century. In 1971, boys' life expectancy at birth was only 69, compared with 72 in 1985, and girls' expectancy was 75 in 1971 compared with 77 in 1985.

SOURCE: Government Actuary's Department.

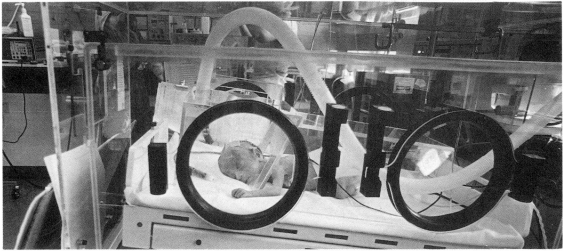

**Neo-natal unit, Kings College Hospital**

# INFANT MORTALITY

## 6,906
### infant deaths (UK, 1986)
### (9.5 per 1,000 live births)

## 4,000
### still births (UK, 1986)
### (5 per 1,000 live births)

'Infant deaths' covers all children dying in the first year from birth; still births occur after 28 weeks after conception. There has been steady improvement throughout the twentieth century: far fewer mothers as well as infants die now than in 1900. But we still have not reached the standards of many European countries.

## Who?

**M/F.**   Girls outlive boys through infancy as well as the rest of life. Their infant mortality rate is 8.1 per 1,000 live births against 10.1 for males. At whatever point of infancy you take — from one day to a week to a year — proportionately more females survive.

## When?
This is how infant deaths break down over that first year.

|  | Deaths | Rate per 1,000 live births |
|---|---|---|
| Under one day | 1,750 | 2.4 |
| Between one day and under one week | 1,380 | 1.9 |
| Between one week and under four weeks | 730 | 1.0 |
| Between four weeks and under one year | 3,050 | 4.2 |

## Deaths in childbirth
50 mothers died giving birth, a rate of 0.07 per 1,000 live births.

## International comparison
Several other European countries have a lower infant mortality rate, including France (8.3), Sweden (6.7), and Finland (6.4).

## Trends
Infant mortality is falling both long- and short-term and has fallen fairly steadily throughout this century. It was 142 deaths per 1,000 live births in 1900-02, compared with 16 in 1975, and only 9.5 today. (1986 figures were actually very slightly up on 1985, but this was almost certainly due to an exceptionally cold spell in the early part of the year.) Maternal mortality has fallen from 4.71 per 1,000 live births in 1900-02 to 0.07 in 1986.

SOURCES: Annual Abstract of Statistics 1988; On the State of the Public Health 1987.

# ABORTIONS

## 166,000 abortions (GB, 1987)

**About one in five conceptions** in England and Wales result in abortions. Nevertheless, Britain has one of the lowest abortion rates in the world, around 12 per 1,000 women between the ages of 15 and 44.

Women in Great Britain do not have the right to abortion on demand (and in Northern Ireland abortion is still illegal). They have to gain two doctors' consent on one of four different health grounds; the overwhelming majority of abortions are carried out because of 'risk to the physical or mental health of the woman'. Not all doctors will give their consent and women may be forced to travel outside their own area for an abortion. In addition, red tape and waiting lists may protract an unwanted pregnancy.

Source: Social Trends 1988; Birth Control Trust.

## Who?

34% of all teenage conceptions in England and Wales in 1986 were aborted (40,460). Teenagers also make up about 38% of those having late abortions — because they often take no action until after about 15 weeks have elapsed.

Source: OPCS.

## Where?

In 1986, 49% of abortions in Great Britain were conducted at NHS hospitals, 51% in private hospitals and clinics. In 1971, NHS hospitals accounted for 59%. Women choose private hospitals for various reasons, including their local doctor's refusal of permission, long waiting lists, and a desire for superior facilities and treatment.

## Why?

One possible cause of the recent increase in abortions is that fewer women have been using the Pill since the health risks (which have been disputed) were publicised in 1983.

A Cosmopolitan survey in October 1988 of 21,000 single women — 14% of whom had had abortions — found that only one in five of these was the result of casual sex. In most cases, the father was the woman's regular partner.

> Nearly 90% of sexually active women were using some sort of contraception in 1983.

## Late abortions

In 1987, 1,660 abortions (1% of the total) were carried out after the twentieth completed week of pregnancy. About half are on teenagers. According to a report on 'Late Abortions in England and Wales' by the Royal College of Obstetricians and Gynaecologists in 1984, a significant number are due to avoidable delays and deficiencies in NHS organisation.

Sources: Co-Ordinating Committee in Defence of the 1967 Abortion Act; Social Trends 1989.

## Deaths

The 1967 Abortion Act has certainly saved mothers' lives. 110 maternal deaths attributable to abortion were recorded between 1952 and 1955 and only six between 1983 and 1985.

## Trends

Both the short- and long-term trends in Britain are upwards. Abortions have risen steadily since 1983, and sharply over the last two decades:

1971 — 101,000 Abortions
1981 — 139,000 Abortions

SOURCES: Social Trends 1988; Social Trends 1989; Birth Control Trust.

**Demonstration against the Alton Abortion Bill, January 1988**

# SUICIDES

## You could have caught her weeks before the camera did.

To give money to the Samaritans phone 01-200 0200.

## 4,839 suicides (UK, 1986)

Suicides may well be higher than the official figure, because coroners cannot always determine whether there was a serious attempt to commit suicide. Suicide methods can to some extent be controlled — eliminating carbon monoxide from domestic gas supplies helped cut down suicide rates in the 1960s; restricting the availability of painkillers in chemists and supermarkets and educating people to throw away unwanted medicines may help now. The telephone counselling service offered by the Samaritans has clearly helped many people but has not had a demonstrable effect on suicide rates.

The Samaritans themselves stress that it is often possible to identify likely suicide cases.

### Who?

**M/F.** Roughly twice as many men commit suicide as women:

2,839 men (England and Wales, 1987)
1,147 women

Men are more likely to gas or hang themselves. Women are more likely to take poison.

**Class.** Suicide occurs in all groups in society; none is particularly at risk.

**Marital status.** Most suicides occur among the single, divorced and widowed.

**Age.** In 1987 suicide was most common among men aged 25-34. But the general pattern is that total suicides for the different age groups between 25 and 64 remain roughly equal in numbers. The suicide *rate* though is currently highest among men over 60. Women commit most suicides after the age of 45.

### How?

People use many methods to kill themselves. The most favoured seem to be poisoning by gases and vapours (accounting for 1,000 suicides in 1985), car exhaust gassing (900 suicides), and hanging (over 1,000). 192 suffocated themselves with a plastic bag. 200 jumped off 'high places'.

### When?

Most suicides occur not in the dark, gloomy months but in April, May and June.

# PARASUICIDES

## 200,000 parasuicides every year

Parasuicide is an act of self-injury, classically of overdosing, which can lead to death, but is not a truly deliberate attempt to kill oneself. Usually it is a way of seeking attention, and is particularly common among the young. Parasuicides create a considerable burden on the NHS, and do indeed sometimes lead to death.

### Who?

**M/F.** Women are much more likely to commit parasuicide, especially adolescents — every year about 1 in 100 girls between 15-19 overdose.

**Age.** Parasuicide, unlike suicide, is most common among young adults.

---

## Samaritans

In 1987, the Samaritans received well over two million calls, a third of them serious. The Samaritans also stress that it's a myth that suicides don't talk about it beforehand — most give definite warnings of their intentions. According to one report, most suicides have had a depressive illness in the past and have visited their GP in the month beforehand. 40%, in addition, have a history of parasuicide.

Source: Suicide and Deliberate Self-harm, Office of Health Economics 1981.

## Trends

Over the last 50 years suicides have gone up and down between 4,000 and 6,000. In 1938, for example, the figure was 5,794. One noticeable trend since the mid-1970s has been a steady rise in suicides among men of working age which closely paralleled the increase in unemployment.

SOURCES: Mortality Statistics, England and Wales, 1985, OPCS; Samaritans; ed. Alwyn Smith and Bobbie Jacobson, The Nation's Health 1988.

**Class.** The long-term unemployed are about 11 times more likely to commit parasuicide than most other groups.

### How?

The most common method is self-poisoning with drugs — over 100,000 men and women are treated in hospital for this, every year. It's the most common reason for acute admission of women to hospital and the second most common (after heart disease) for men. 90% of all attempts involve overdosing, mainly with analgesics or minor tranquillisers. Perhaps parasuicides could be prevented by avoiding unnecessary tranquilliser prescriptions.

## Consequences

**Hospital admissions.** Parasuicide accounts for 10% of all admissions to hospital, and is the second commonest reason for emergency medical admission. Many parasuicides, though, are not referred to hospital, but treated at home by GPs.

Source: Suicide and Deliberate Self-harm, Office of Health Economics 1981.

**Deaths.** One estimate is that around 500 to 600 parasuicides die every year.

## Trends

In the three decades before 1977 there was a very sharp rise in hospital discharge rates for parasuicide among women — for example, from less than 0.5 per 100 women aged 15-24 before 1952 to more than five per 100 by 1977. Rates fell thereafter till 1982 (when the rate for 15-24-year-olds was approaching four per 100), and appear to have kept falling.

Source: M.R. Alderson, 'National trends in self poisoning in women', The Lancet, 1985, 27 April: 974-975.

SOURCE: Samaritans.

# ACCIDENTS

## Fatal accidents in England and Wales in 1985

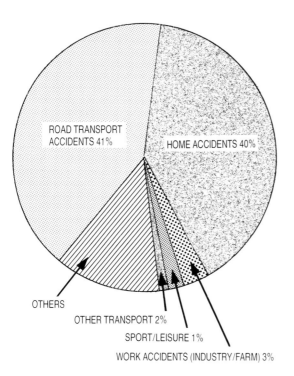

ROAD TRANSPORT ACCIDENTS 41%

HOME ACCIDENTS 40%

OTHERS

OTHER TRANSPORT 2%

SPORT/LEISURE 1%

WORK ACCIDENTS (INDUSTRY/FARM) 3%

Sources: OPCS Mortality Statistics, Home Accident Surveillance System.

These comparative statistics give a good idea of where most accidents continue to take place. What is perhaps surprising is how dangerous the home can be, and how the workplace is much less dangerous. It's also notable how road accidents dwarf all other forms of transport.

### Class

The Black Report pointed out that **poorer socio-economic groups are much more vulnerable to accidents**. Boys in class V had a 10 times greater chance of dying from fire, falls or drowning than those in class I, and a *seven* times greater chance of dying as pedestrians. Such a high incidence rate is linked to poor supervision and homes with less safe furnishing, heating and domestic appliances.

Source: ed. Peter Townsend and Nick Davidson, Inequalities in Health, The Black Report 1982.

### Compensation

How much compensation should be paid out in damages if people suffer injury or death through others' negligence? The Citizen Action Compensation Campaign believes that awards are far too small and wrongly set by precedent, and that it takes far too long to bring cases to court. 'Today's derisory award becomes tomorrow's even more derisory award,' says Campaign leader Des Wilson. Only £3,500 was awarded in 1989 for the death of an 11-year-old girl through a wrongly administered injection. Damages awarded in the courts in 1988 ranged from £1,750-75,000 for eye injuries and £1,100-53,126 for knee injuries.

Source: Observer, 26.2.1989.

### Trends

Life is steadily becoming safer in most respects. In 1987, the total of accidental deaths in Great Britain was down 32% on 1971, and accidents at home and on the roads had fallen by similar amounts.

Source: Social Trends 1989.

## TRANSPORT ACCIDENTS (UK, 1976–86)

It's very clear which are the most dangerous forms of travel in order, apart from sea vs bus/coach. The above figures, though, for the 10-year period, 1976-86, are a little misleading. A fair comparison of air and road travel should include all aircraft casualties, including light planes and helicopters and not just passenger services.

# TRANSPORT ACCIDENTS

## Fatal casualties

Ironically, although you are much less likely to have an accident with certain forms of transport, you are much more likely to die if you do get into an accident. 60% of casualties in the air die, compared with 4% at sea, 3% on rail, 2% on cars and motorbikes, 1% on pedal cycles and 0.3% on buses and coaches.

## Trends

In general there have been too many fluctuations between 1976 and 1986 to pick out clear trends, apart from a fall in recent years in car and motorbike deaths.

Sources: Transport Statistics, 1976-86, Department of Transport; Social Trends 1989.

|  | Aeroplanes | Rail | Sea | Road | | | |
|---|---|---|---|---|---|---|---|
|  |  |  |  | Bus/Coach | Cars | Cyclists | Motorbikes |
| Deaths (per billion passenger kilometres) | 0.3 | 0.3 | 1.8 | 0.8 | 5.9 | 68 | 156 |
| Total casualties | 0.5 | 10.6 | 41.1 | 240 | 382 | 6,024 | 10,245 |

Source: Transport Statistics, 1976-86, Department of Transport.

**M1 plane crash, January 1989**

# ROAD ACCIDENTS

**Multi-vehicle pile-up, M25 in Kent**

**5,125
deaths (GB, 1987)
64,293
seriously injured
242,055
slightly injured**

There were 239,063 road accidents in Britain in 1987. As a nation, we are more careful drivers than most, and have considerably improved over the last two decades. But we still sustain more road casualties each year than we might in a minor war. Driving habits — especially the level of drink-driving — could be improved much further.

# ROAD ACCIDENTS

## How?
It is very dangerous to be a **pedestrian** — 1,703 were killed in 1987, compared with 2,206 drivers and passengers of cars and taxis, 723 riders of motorbikes and other 'two-wheeled motor vehicles' and 280 cyclists.

## Most dangerous transport. The top five killers are:

| | deaths | vehicles involved (per 100 million km travelled) |
|---|---|---|
| 1. Motorbikes, mopeds (two-wheeled motor vehicles) | 12.7 | 920 |
| 2. Pedal cycles | 6.4 | 619 |
| 3. Cars and taxis | 0.5 | 112 |
| 4. Light goods vehicles | 0.3 | 85 |
| 5. Heavy goods vehicles | 0.3 | 64 |

The heavier your vehicle, by and large, the safer you would seem to be.

## Who?

**Age.** The most vulnerable age group in terms of killed and seriously injured is 15-19-year-olds, with 13,752 casualties. **Road deaths in 1986 caused 34% of all deaths in the 15-24 age group**.

## When?
The largest numbers of casualties occur in the peak traffic rush hours, first, between 5 pm and 6 pm, and second, between 8 am and 9 am. Adult casualties are almost as high late-night, between 11 pm and midnight. Child casualties peak around the end of the school day between 3 pm and 4 pm, reaching a secondary peak around lunchtime.

## Where?
Motorways are not as dangerous as you might think — a car driver was 3.8 times more likely to have a fatal or serious injury on an A-road in 1986.

## Cost
The cost of a fatal road accident in 1987 was estimated at just over £555,000 including the value of lost output, damage to property, medical, police and insurance administration costs, plus allowance for suffering.

## Drink-driving
**Drivers or riders were over the alcohol limit in about 20% of fatal accidents**.

## International comparison
Great Britain has one of the lowest rates of road death in the western world. In 1985, for example, the rate of 9.4 deaths per 100,000 population was better than Japan and Germany, with 10.0 each, and much better than the USA (18), France (20.7), or Portugal (30.2).

## Trends
The long-term trends in road accidents are definitely down. Since 1977, deaths have fallen 23% from 6,614, and the total number of road accidents has fallen by 10% from 265,861.

SOURCES: Social Trends 1988, 1989; Annual Abstract of Statistics 1989; Road Transport Statistics; Department of Transport.

# RAILWAY ACCIDENTS

## 103 deaths (GB, 1987)
## 9,800 injured

Three serious railway accidents at Clapham Junction, Purley and Glasgow between December 1988 and March 1989, resulting in 42 deaths, have posed major questions about the safety of British Rail. Critics argue that managers have paid too much attention to economy and efficiency, and too little to safety. Clapham Junction was the most glaring example — 35 people died because a wire in a signal system shorted, having been left bare by overworked, underpaid technicians.

But by comparison with other forms of transport, railway accidents are relatively rare. In 1987 only 11 people were killed in actual train accidents. Most injuries and deaths came about in 'other accidents through movement of railways vehicles', which include entering or alighting from trains, opening or closing carriage doors at stations, and 'accidents on railway premises', which include ascending or descending steps at stations.

## Where?

**Train accidents** where people were actually travelling, resulted in 11 deaths and 396 people injured in 1987.

**Other accidents through movement of railway vehicles** produced 57 deaths and 2,777 injuries.

**Accidents on railways premises** produced a higher-than-usual total of 35 deaths, and more usual total of 6,627 injuries.

## Train accidents

There were 1,166 train accidents in all, including 290 collisions and 192 derailments. 392 involved running into level-crossing gates and other obstructions.

## Human error

792 train drivers went through signals at red in 1987, according to a confidential report compiled by BR's safety director Maurice Holmes, and forwarded to the Railway Inspectorate Advisory Committee.

Source: Evening Standard, 7.3.1989.

---

**316 railway suicides** (GB, 1987)

It's remarkable how many people choose to follow Anna Karenina and commit suicide in front of trains. The figure has remained fairly constant, too, varying between 2196 and 369 since 1977. Such suicides can cause great anguish to the drivers involved. One had nightmares for a year after. Another went home and didn't come out of the house for four months. By July 1989, all train drivers will be entitled under the amended Criminal Injuries Compensation Act to compensation for shock when they run someone over.

---

SOURCES: Department of Transport; Annual Abstract of Statistics 1989.

# RAILWAY ACCIDENTS

**Clapham train disaster, December 1988**

# AIR ACCIDENTS

## No deaths (GB, 1987)
## 10 seriously injured
## 45 killed in helicopter accidents

Air accidents and explosions seem to attract the most headlines. The Manchester aircraft fire of 1985, and the Lockerbie tragedy at the end of 1988, when 240 people in a Pan Am jet were blown out of the sky, are two spectacular examples.

In fact, aeroplanes, with the possible exception of helicopters, are by far the safest way to travel. But recent defects in equipment and ageing aeroplanes have highlighted the need for constant vigilance, and helicopters still present safety challenges (although 43 of the above deaths came in a single accident at Sumborough to a helicopter carrying North Sea oil workers).

## Total distance travelled
In 1986, UK airline passengers travelled over 85 BILLION passenger kilometres, both nationally and internationally, with none being killed.

## Trends
Air casualties can vary considerably, but it is not unusual for there to be no fatalities — the total was the same again in 1987.

Source: Department of Transport.

**Lockerbie after the disaster, December 1988**

# ACCIDENTS AT SEA

## 206 killed (UK, 1987)

Deaths and injuries at sea have fluctuated substantially over the years, and it is difficult to perceive definite trends. But there is concern that they may escalate. Six coastguard stations have been shut since 1979, leaving 22 stations to guard 6,000 miles of coastline. Coastguard staff have been cut from 700 to 500, despite a 1979 Department of Transport recommendation that 671 were needed for efficient operation of their services. A Don't Sink the Coastguard campaign petition, signed by over 25,000 fishermen, mariners, and coastal dwellers, calling for stations to be reopened was presented to John Prescott, Shadow Transport Secretary, on 14 March 1989.

189 lives were also lost when the Herald of Free Enterprise sank at Zeebrugge; they are not included because this took place off the coast of Belgium, rather than in coastal waters of the UK.

## Causes

There is no one single outstanding cause of deaths at sea. In 1987, 31 persons were lost overboard. Others died in incidents swimming (10), diving (8), and falling off cliffs (11), and on all kinds of craft, from fishing vessels (7) to powered pleasure craft (15), small craft (4), and a sailboard (1). There were 5,563 search-and-rescue- operations in 1987.

## Trends

Since 1976 the total of lives lost at sea has fluctuated between a high of 484 in 1985 and a low of 181 in 1982. The total for 1988 will probably be high again as a result of the Piper Alpha oil platform disaster in which over 150 were killed.

Source: Transport Statistics, 1976-86; HM Coastguard Incident Statistics, Department of Transport.

**Herald of Free Enterprise, Zeebrugge, March 1987**

# ACCIDENTS IN THE HOME

## 4,980 deaths (GB, 1987) 3,100,000 non-fatal accidents (GB, 1986)

A casual glance at the figures and you could argue that it's almost as dangerous to be at home as on the roads. Home accidents account for about 40% of all fatal accidents, and a third of accidents treated in hospital.

## Treatment

Of an estimated 3,100,000 non-fatal accidents in 1986, 900,000 were treated by a general practitioner, and 2,200,000 by an accident and emergency department in a hospital. But of these, 92% were not admitted for treatment, and only 5% were admitted to the hospital for an average stay of 11 days.

## Causes

Falls are the most common cause of accidents. The main causes of accidents treated in hospital in England and Wales in 1987 were:

| | |
|---|---|
| Falls | 39.3% |
| Struck by object/person | 18.9% |
| Cutting/piercing | 17.2% |
| Foreign body | 4.6% |
| Burning | 4.4% |
| Poisoning | 1.9% |

Electric currents, which might be considered more dangerous, only accounted in 1986 for 0.09% of accidents.

**Poisoning.** An estimated 30,000 children a year are involved in accidental poisonings. One study of under-5s showed that medicinal products were involved in 59% of cases (nearly 75% for 1- and 2-year-olds), and household or garden chemicals in 37%. Unsafe storage and inadequate supervision of children were highlighted as major avoidable factors.

Source: On the State of the Public Health 1987.

## Who?

**Age.** Young children, under 5, and those 65 and over, have by far the most home accidents — 24% and 12% respectively in 1986. The young and elderly are the groups most vulnerable to falls — 43% of children under 15, and 76% of women over 75 who were treated for accidents had had falls.

## When?

Peak-times for accidents are when the home is most populated — on a Sunday, and between 4.00 pm and 8.00 pm.

## Trends

Fatal home accidents in England and Wales have decreased fairly steadily from over 7,000 in the mid-1960s to 5,000-6,000 in the 1970s to 4,000-5,000 in the 1980s and were amongst the lowest in Europe in 1986. But there has been no marked change in the estimated number of non-fatal home accidents since 1980.

---

## Fires

957 people died in fires in the United Kingdom in 1986; there were 12,770 casualties. Of 387,000 reported fires, 63,000 were in dwellings, where the commonest cause was the unintentional misuse of appliances, such as leaving a fire on.

---

SOURCES:Home Accident Surveillance System 1986 (10th Annual Report) and 1987; Social Trends 1989.

# ACCIDENTS AT WORK

## 525
## died (GB, 1987-88)
## 33,746 major injuries

While work injuries and fatalities occur less often than accidents at home, there are many work sectors where accidents continue to happen unnecessarily, particularly construction.

## Which industries?

The most fatal industries in 1987-88 were construction (157 deaths), manufacturing (100 deaths), transport and communication (55 deaths), and agriculture, forestry and fishing (55 deaths). There were only five deaths in banking and finance.

> A study of work accidents showed that 'in nearly 70 per cent of these fatal accidents, positive management action could have saved lives'.
>
> Source: Deadly Maintenance: A Study of Fatal Accidents at Work, Health and Safety Executive 1985.

Michael Meacher, Shadow Minister of Employment, pointed out at the end of 1988 that nearly three workers are killed on construction sites every week, not because of new technology, but from the same causes as in the last century, such as falling off ladders and being suffocated in trenches.

More detailed analysis of 1986-87 injuries to employees shows that out of 161,000 injuries to employees, the main causes were:

| | |
|---|---|
| Injured whilst handling, lifting or carrying | 46,000 |
| Slip, trip or fall on same level | 29,000 |
| Struck by moving, flying or falling object | 22,000 |
| Falls from a height | 15,000 |

Source: Health and Safety Executive, Health and Safety Council Annual Report 1986-87.

## Trends

Fatalities at work have been on a downward trend, apart from the odd oscillation, since the 1960s. A major factor in recent years has been the decline of the more physically dangerous manufacturing sector, and the growth of service industries.

Source: Health and Safety Executive.

# FATAL DISEASES

**Deaths in the UK (1986)**

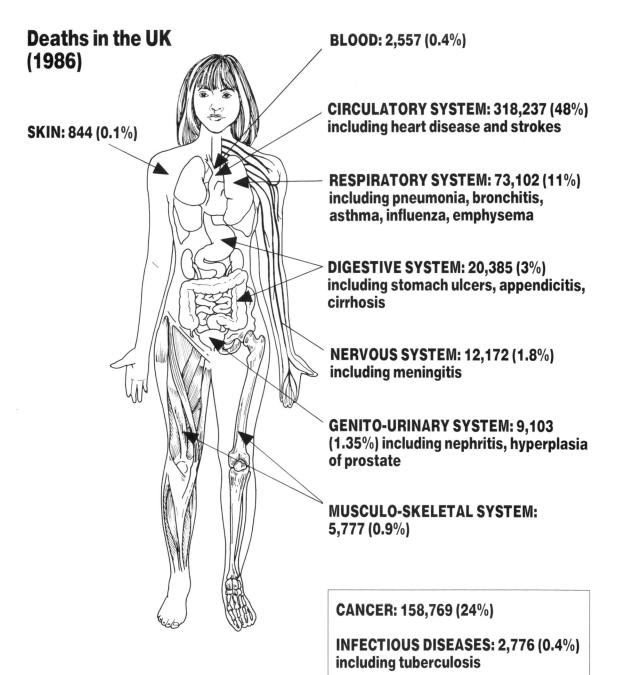

**BLOOD: 2,557 (0.4%)**

**SKIN: 844 (0.1%)**

**CIRCULATORY SYSTEM: 318,237 (48%) including heart disease and strokes**

**RESPIRATORY SYSTEM: 73,102 (11%) including pneumonia, bronchitis, asthma, influenza, emphysema**

**DIGESTIVE SYSTEM: 20,385 (3%) including stomach ulcers, appendicitis, cirrhosis**

**NERVOUS SYSTEM: 12,172 (1.8%) including meningitis**

**GENITO-URINARY SYSTEM: 9,103 (1.35%) including nephritis, hyperplasia of prostate**

**MUSCULO-SKELETAL SYSTEM: 5,777 (0.9%)**

**CANCER: 158,769 (24%)**

**INFECTIOUS DISEASES: 2,776 (0.4%) including tuberculosis**

SOURCE: Annual Abstract of Statistics 1988

# FATAL DISEASES

There are three main killers among the major groups of diseases:

- **diseases of the circulatory system, including heart disease and strokes, which together account for nearly HALF of all deaths;**
- **cancers, which account for nearly a QUARTER of deaths;**
- **and diseases of the respiratory system, accounting for just over a TENTH of deaths.**

Other areas of the body, such as the digestive, genito-urinary and musculo-skeletal systems, barely feature by comparison. And infectious diseases, such as tuberculosis, which used to ravage society, have almost disappeared.

The main killers now are 'diseases of civilization', which are largely absent among primitive societies, and whose incidence has steadily increased in most countries in line with economic growth. They can be linked to a poor diet (including alcohol and fatty foods), lack of exercise, smoking and poor environment (particularly urban and industrial pollution). All of these are factors that can be controlled.

Most diseases have a higher incidence among the poor.

Source: Annual Abstract of Statistics 1988.

## HEART DISEASE: 181,491 deaths*

Heart disease is responsible for heart attacks, when the blood supply to the heart muscle is interrupted.

## Risk factors
High blood cholesterol, a fatty diet combined with lack of exercise, smoking.

## Who?

**M/F.** Heart disease led to 89,000 deaths among men (31% of all male deaths) in England and Wales, and 74,000 deaths among women (24% of all female deaths).

**Age.** Heart disease was responsible for the premature deaths of about 24,000 men between 35 and 64 in 1986.

**Class.** Male manual workers are actually over three and a half times more likely to die of heart disease than professional men, although this has long been thought of as the disease of the workaholic executive.

Source: G. Rose and M.G. Marmot, 'Social class and coronary heart disease', British Heart Journal, 1981, 45:13-19.

## Trends
There has been a slow decline in heart disease since the 1970s — due partly to improvements in national diet (less fatty foods) and to reduced smoking.

Source: Social Trends 1988.

*UK, 1986

# FATAL DISEASES

## STROKES:
## 82,052 deaths*

Strokes occur when the blood supply to the brain is interrupted — usually when a blood vessel is blocked by a clot, or bursts. About one in 500 people a year have strokes.

### Fatality rate
Roughly a third of people who have strokes die; one third suffer disabilities; one third make a complete recovery.

### Risk factors
High blood pressure, smoking, high cholesterol levels in the blood, and diabetes.

## PNEUMONIA:
## 33,467 deaths*

Pneumonia involves acute lung inflammation and can result in death within weeks. The aged are particularly at risk, whereas the young and middle-aged usually survive attacks. It is also associated with smoking and urban pollution. Legionnaire's disease is a notorious form of pneumonia although it only accounts for around 2% of pneumonia deaths in Britain.

## CHRONIC LUNG DISEASE:
## 15,284 deaths*

Chronic lung disease (including bronchitis, emphysema and asthma) involves a long and gradual deterioration of the lungs and their functioning. We have a very high rate of what has been known as the English disease.

### Risk factors
The disease is more common where it is rainier and colder — further north, especially the North West. It's often associated with cold, damp housing, and is more common in smokers.

## Top 10 killers (UK, 1986)

| | |
|---|---:|
| Heart disease | 181,491 |
| Strokes | 82,052 |
| Lung cancer | 40,142 |
| Pneumonia | 33,467 |
| Breast cancer | 15,366 |
| Chronic lung disease (bronchitis, emphysema, asthma) | 15,284 |
| Mental disorders | 13,423 |
| Colon cancer | 12,524 |
| Stomach cancer | 10,918 |
| Diabetes | 8,515 |

Sources: Annual Abstract of Statistics 1988; Cancer Research Campaign

*UK, 1986

# CANCERS:
# 158,769 deaths*

Cancer is now responsible for about a quarter of all deaths. It is estimated that one in three people will develop cancer at some time in their life. There are over 150 different types, some of which can be treated successfully.

## Risk factors
30% of all cancer deaths are attributable to *smoking*, not just lung cancer but also cancers of the mouth, pharynx, larynx, oesophagus, bladder, and other regions.

## Fatality rates
The five-year survival rate for patients first diagnosed in England and Wales in 1981 is as follows:

| | |
|---|---|
| Pancreas | 4% |
| Lung | 7-8% |
| Stomach | 10-11% |
| Colon | 37-38% |
| Prostate | 43% |
| Cervix | 58% |
| Breast | 62% |
| Skin (excluding melanoma) | 97% |
| All cancers | 40% |
|     all men | 35% |
|     all women | 46% |

Source: Cancer Research Campaign.

*UK, 1986

**Lung cancer cell**

# CANCER

## BREAST CANCER:
## 15,366 deaths*

This is the commonest female cancer death and the commonest cause of all deaths in women between the ages of 35-53, except in Scotland where more now die from lung cancer.

### Causes
The earlier a woman starts menstruating and the later she reaches menopause, the greater the risk of breast cancer. Rich diet which helps bring on menstruation also contributes. (Women have been menstruating earlier and earlier this century with steadily improving diet).

### Class
The rich are more vulnerable than the poor. The Standard Mortality Ratio is 121 for women in socio-economic Class I, and only 78 in Class V.

### International comparison
The UK has the world's highest breast cancer mortality rate. It is estimated that 1 in 15 women will develop breast cancer at some time in their life.

Source: Royal College of General Practitioners 1988.

## CANCER OF THE COLON:
## 12,524 deaths*

Bowel cancer, which includes cancers of the colon, rectum and anus, mainly affects people over 40. A high-fat, high-meat, low-fibre diet is thought to play a part. There was a sharp fall in deaths in the UK between 1942 and 1962, which may be due to a sharp rise in dietary fibre intake during the war when cereal consumption more than doubled. Trials are currently underway to see whether screening for bowel cancer could help prevent more deaths — chances of survival are 90% if tumours are diagnosed in early stages as against 30% at five years.

### Trends
Death rates from bowel cancer have changed little over the last decade, although there is evidence of a slow decline in mortality among women.

Source: ed. Alwyn Smith and Bobbie Jacobson, The Nation's Health, 1988.

## STOMACH CANCER:
## 10,918 deaths*

Stomach cancer is often only caught in the late stages, since the early symptoms, which include loss of appetite, are not obvious. It occurs mainly in the over-50s.

### Causes
The most likely causes are too little fresh fruit and vegetables, and too much salt. The poorer the diet, the greater the risk of stomach cancer.

### International comparison
The stomach cancer mortality rate here is roughly twice that of the USA.

### Trends
The incidence of stomach cancer has been steadily declining since the 1950s, from 30 to 20 per 100,000, presumably due to improved diet.

*UK, 1986

## CERVICAL CANCER:
## 2,203 deaths*

Cervical cancer has probably attracted more attention than other cancers with higher mortality rates — perhaps because it is generally agreed to be a preventable disease.

### Who?

**Age.**   In 1984, when the total of deaths was 2,126, women over 55 accounted for over 70% of deaths, women under 44 for 17%.

### Causes

There is strong evidence that cervical cancer is sexually transmissible and that the agents are variants of the human papilloma virus (HPV) which can cause genital warts. There are a variety of risk factors including smoking and use of the Pill.

### Trends

Overall mortality has decreased somewhat from 2,551 deaths in 1971 to 2,203 in 1986. Smears examined in the same period were increased from 2,205,000 to 4,270,000. But death rates among 25—34-year-olds rose between 1970 and 1982, and it has been estimated that 4,000 women will die every year by the year 2000.

Sources: Social Trends 1988; ed. Alwyn Smith and Bobbie Jacobson, The Nation's Health 1988.

## LUNG CANCER:
## 40,142 deaths*

This is the greatest killer of all cancers. The more urbanised an area, the more it kills. Lung cancer has led to nearly a million premature deaths in the last 50 years.

### Who?

**M/F.**   Lung cancer led to 28,632 deaths among men (35% of all male cancer deaths — 1986) and 11,511 deaths among women (15% of all female cancer deaths).

### Causes

Over 90% of lung cancer deaths are attributable to smoking.

### Trends

Since 1951, lung cancer death rates have doubled for men (from 51 per million population to 102 in 1987) and quadrupled for women (from nine to nearly 41 per million population). Since 1979, the rate has been slowly falling in men, while continuing to rise among women. Lung cancer replaced breast cancer as the major cancer killer of women in Scotland in 1985, and looks likely to do so soon in England and Wales.

Source: Social Trends 1988, 1989.

*UK, 1986

# AIDS

**1,116**
**deaths (UK, to March 1989)**
**2,103**
**cases reported**
**9,617**
**HIV positive (up to January 1989)**

At the time of writing, we still don't know how serious an epidemic AIDS really is in Britain. Some estimate that for every case reported, 50 people could be invisibly infected. Social Trends 1988 estimated on the basis of 1,000 reported cases, that there were between 35,000 and 55,000 unreported ones. The difficulty in making any estimate is that the precise incubation period for AIDS is still not known — it is thought to be between five and 10 years. We also don't know how many people found HIV positive, i.e. infected with the HIV virus, will actually develop full-blown AIDS.

In order to determine the full extent of the AIDS virus, in November 1988 Minister of Health Kenneth Clarke gave the go-ahead for anonymous testing of blood samples taken from hospitals — without the donors' knowledge.

## Who?
Around 90 per cent of all AIDS cases, including deaths, are homosexual men. There are still very few women with AIDS. Drug users taking drugs intravenously are a much greater proportion of AIDS cases in the USA, and may come to be here too, though drugs are a much more widespread problem there.

| | | |
|---|---|---|
| Homo/bisexuals: | 1,726 cases, | 906 deaths. |
| Heterosexuals: | 84 cases, | 37 deaths. |
| Drug Abusers: | 76 cases, | 37 deaths. |
| Haemophiliacs: | | 84 deaths. |
| Recipients of blood: | | 27 deaths. |
| Children of At-Risk/Infected Parents: | | 10 deaths. |

## Fatality rate
Roughly 50% of AIDS cases die within one year of diagnosis, and 30% die within two or three years of diagnosis.

## Regions
The highest incidence of people reported HIV positive as of August 1988 was in the North West Thames area — 2,410. England as a whole had 7,130, Scotland 1,504, Wales and Northern Ireland only 113 and 47 respectively. Scotland is notable because 12% of the total AIDS cases in 1988 were female, and 55% of all HIV positive cases were intravenous drug misusers — both very high compared with the national percentages.

Source: Scottish Education Dept. Social Work Group 1988 and Hansard 8.6.88.

SOURCE: AIDS Unit, Department of Health.

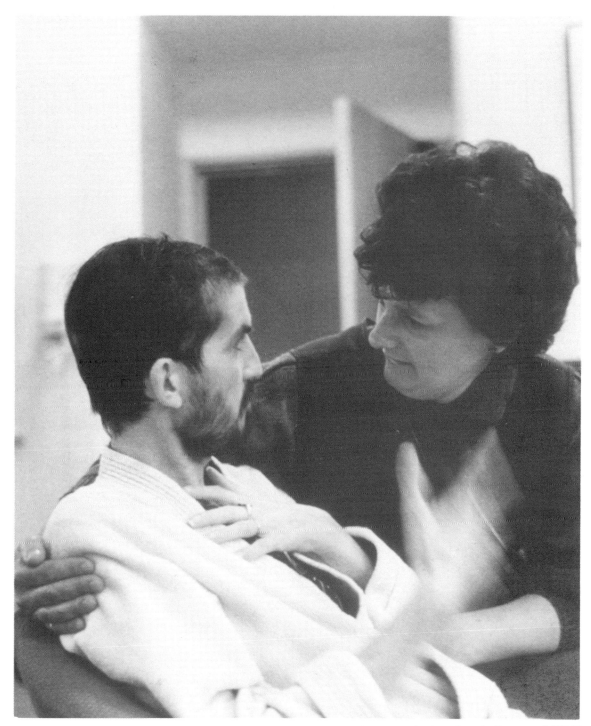

**Resident at London Lighthouse 'a centre for those facing the challenge of AIDS'**

# THE DISABLED

**Stoke Mandeville Hospital**

## 6,202,000
## disabled adults (UK, 1987)

The survey of disabled adults in the UK conducted by the Office of Population Censuses and Surveys, and published in November 1988, produced a shock. The total number of disabled is roughly *twice* what most people had thought (and that doesn't include disabled *children*). The OPCS results correspond roughly with a MORI survey conducted in 1987 for the Spastics Society which showed that about one in 10 people suffer from some disability. The General Household Survey 1985 found that even more — 20.8% of adults in private households — had a long-standing health problem or disability, but cannot be considered so reliable.

It is easy to ignore the disabled — they are often shut off and out of the way. But they constitute one of the greatest and least acknowledged of social problems. And, not surprisingly, one of their most passionate desires is to be fully accepted into normal, social life.

## Who?

**Age.**　There are approximately *2 million disabled under the age of 60*. The majority, though, are elderly: 1.2 million are aged 60-70, and 3 million are over 70.

Only 2% of 16-19-year-olds have a disability, compared with 13% of 50-59 year olds and 71% of over-80's. The majority of severely handicapped are also over 70.

**M/F.**　There are more disabled women (3,656,000) than men (2,544,000). Partly this is because they live longer. **About 1,500,000 women aged 75 or over have disabilities compared with just over 600,000 men**.

# THE DISABLED

## Where?

**Homes.**   400,000 (7%) live in some kind of communal establishment. The majority are women and 200,000 are 80 or over. (Only 2% of all adults live in communal establishments, and many are there because they are disabled.)

**Regions.**   Broadly, Wales, the North, Yorkshire and Humberside and Scotland have the highest rates of disabled, while the Greater London area, the South East and East Anglia have the lowest — from 162 per 1,000 population in the North to 119 in Greater London.

## What's the Distinction? Impairment — Disability — Handicap

These three terms are often used interchangeably. But there are differences. Basically an impairment refers to parts or systems of the body not working, disability to activities people cannot perform, handicap to complex roles in relation to people or particular environments.

The survey on disability by the Office of Population Censuses and Surveys gives these examples of differences:

| IMPAIRMENT | DISABILITY | HANDICAP |
|---|---|---|
| Vision | Seeing | Orientation |
| Skeletal | Walking | Mobility |

The same survey found that disabled people find it easier to think, and answer questions in terms of, disability than impairment.

## 498,864 wheelchairs were in use in England in 1987.

Nearly half a million wheelchairs as well as pedal hand-propelled tricycles have been issued under the National Health Service, and many more will have been bought privately. Wheelchair-bound Tracey Booth, leader of the Campaign for Accessible Transport, complains that she can't use any of London's 'so-called public transport'. But 'there's no reason why buses can't be made wheelchair-accessible. They've done this in New York and in other American and European cities'. The number of wheelchairs on issue has risen very steadily more than doubling from 222,740 in 1977.

Source: Health and Personal Social Services for England 1988; Evening Standard, 23.5.89.

## Numbers affected by disabilities

| | |
|---|---|
| LOCOMOTION | 4,332,000 |
| REACHING AND STRETCHING | 1,230,000 |
| DEXTERITY | 1,737,000 |
| SEEING | 1,668,000 |
| HEARING | 2,588,000 |
| PERSONAL CARE | 2,483,000 |
| CONTINENCE | 1,142,000 |
| COMMUNICATION | 1,202,000 |
| BEHAVIOUR | 1,347,000 |
| INTELLECTUAL FUNCTIONING | 1,475,000 |
| CONSCIOUSNESS | 229,000 |
| EATING, DRINKING, DIGESTING | 276,000 |
| DISFIGUREMENT | 391,000 |

SOURCE: survey, The Prevalence of Disability Among Adults, OPCS, November 1988.

# THE DISABLED

## Severity of disability

Disability is rarely clear-cut. It is a continuum of severity, with many people disabled in more ways than one. The OPCS survey identifies 10 levels of disability and provides 'pen pictures' of typical cases:

**Level 1:** A man, 59, deaf in one ear, has difficulty hearing someone talking in a normal voice in a quiet room.

**Level 2:** A man, 75, often forgets what he was doing, or loses track of what's being said in the middle of a conversation. He has poor hearing and can sit for hours doing nothing.

**Level 6:** A woman, 40, is epileptic, cannot read a short article in a paper, is often confused about the time of day, and feels the need to have someone with her all the time.

**Level 10:** A man, 55, is a stroke victim, cannot walk at all, feed himself or get in or out of a chair without help.

| | |
|---|---|
| Level 1 | 1,198,000 |
| Level 2 | 840,000 |
| Level 3 | 750,000 |
| Level 4 | 704,000 |
| Level 5 | 708,000 |
| Level 6 | 545,000 |
| Level 7 | 486,000 |
| Level 8 | 396,000 |
| Level 9 | 365,000 |
| Level 10 | 210,000 |

## Causes

The most common set of causes for disability are musculo-skeletal complaints (including arthritis, rheumatism and back problems) which affect 46% of the disabled in private households. Next come ear complaints affecting 38%, and eye complaints affecting 22%.

Mental disabilities are the most common among those in communal establishments, affecting some 56%, including senile dementia which affects 26%.

## Problems of the disabled

The particular problems and needs of the disabled can often be overlooked. These include:

- **Housing**: has to be specially adapted for the disabled, particularly steps and stairs.
- **Transport**: many disabled people go out rarely, mainly for essential shopping. Nearly half of mothers with a disabled child never travelled on public transport according to one report.
- **Low income**: many disabled are unable to gain employment and rely on State support.
- **Stigma**: many feel that they are classed as inferior even by hospital doctors.
- **Social isolation**: disabled children particularly are much less likely to play and communicate with other children.
- **Media**: disabled people complain that they are poorly represented in the media by comparison with their numbers, and are shown either as heroic figures or passive victims but rarely as complex individuals and equals.

Source: N. Butler et al., Handicapped Children — Their Homes and Life Styles, University of Bristol 1978.

## Social security cuts

Many disabled people, and especially the Disability Alliance and the Spastics Society, are angry about cuts in their benefits in the social security changes of April 1988. Special needs payments for the disabled were replaced by a disability premium which, it is argued, takes no account of different needs and has left many much worse off.

SOURCE: survey, The Prevalence of Disability Among Adults, OPCS, November 1988.

# BLIND

**146,000
blind (UK, 1986)
81,790
partially sighted**

Around 11,000 people are newly registered as blind each year, most of them from degenerative eye diseases which are the inevitable result of ageing. But in some cases, such as glaucoma and diabetic retinopathy, blindness can be prevented if the disease is diagnosed and treated in time.

## Who?

Out of 11,641 people newly registered as blind in England in 1980-81, 9,795 were 65 and over, 1,655 were 16-64, and only 191 were under 15.

SOURCES: DHSS; Health Departments for Scotland, Wales and Northern Ireland; Royal National Institute for the Blind; On the State of the Public Health 1987.

# 11,000
# are both deaf and blind

Deaf-blindness is one of the most extreme combinations of disabilities, and can cause severe communication, developmental and education problems. The number of children born with multiple disabilities is not decreasing, partly perhaps because of medical success in lowering the infant mortality rate.

## Who?

**Age.**  The majority of deaf-blind — around 6,300 — are over 65. But there is also a bulge of deaf-blind people in their early 20s — there are 1,900 in the 16-24 age group — as a result of the rubella epidemic in the 1960s.

**Causes.**  Rubella (German measles) during pregnancy is the largest single cause, but there are others, not all of which have been identified.

SOURCE: SENSE, The National Deaf-Blind and Rubella Association.

## 400,000
## have severe hearing loss (i.e. cannot hear 71-95 decibels)
## 23,000
## have profound hearing loss (i.e. cannot hear 105 decibels)

There are different kinds of hearing loss. Some people have been deaf since infancy — profoundly 'pre-lingually deaf' — others have become profoundly deaf in later life, some are deaf-blind, some merely hard of hearing.

In addition to the above figures it is estimated that:

- 11,800,000 people have mild hearing loss, involving inability to hear noises at 25 and 35 decibels.
- 1,400,000 have moderate hearing loss, and are unable to hear noises at 45 and 65 decibels.

Altogether, about 17% of the adult population have some hearing impairment.

Source: Institute of Hearing Research Data.

## Who?

**Age.** Over three-fifths of people officially registered as deaf or hard of hearing in 1986 were aged 65 and over. 1,269 were under 16.

Source: DHSS.

## Sign language

50,000 deaf people use British Sign Language as their first language i.e. have grown up with it. According to a BBC survey, roughly 3,000,000 people would like to learn sign language. The more people know BSL, the better the spectrum of communication open to deaf people.

## Needs

According to the Royal National Institute for the Deaf, local authorities are providing poorly for the deaf, particularly basic hearing aids — some people can wait for up to three years from initial referral, to fitting and rehabilitation. More telephones could also be adapted for the hearing-impaired.

## Trends

The numbers of the officially *registered* deaf and hard of hearing have nearly doubled in 10 years — up to 97,431 for England in 1986, from 53,003 in 1976. But it's difficult to know how much this is due to a natural increase in numbers, and how much to improved registration efforts.

Source: DHSS.

SOURCE: Royal National Institute for the Deaf.

# DISABILITIES

## 100,000
## have cerebral palsy (UK)

Cerebral palsy is a disorder of movement and posture which comes in many forms and degrees. Some people have a barely perceptible condition, others are unable even to sit. The Spastics Society points out that cerebral palsy is an injury rather than a disease, occurring during the first years of life, involving damage to, or failure to develop, a small part of the brain controlling movement. Speech and hearing can be affected as well as walk and posture. There is no cure, though physiotherapy can help sufferers to rehabilitate.

### Rate
One in 500 babies, roughly, is born with cerebral palsy.

### Causes
There are many causes. Some arise during pregnancy, sometimes a baby's brain is damaged during birth, at other times an illness or brain injury occurs in the first years of life. Not all causes, though, have been identified and there is still much to be discovered.

SOURCE: Spastics Society.

## 50,000
## have multiple sclerosis (UK)

Multiple sclerosis is a disease of gradual wasting away, which destroys the covering of nerves in the central nervous system (but not, curiously, peripheral nerves). It leads most commonly to muscle weakness, sometimes paralysis, slurred speech and visual impairment. Attacks come and go over many years.

'You learn one day that you can no longer turn the pages of a book; you start to worry whether you'll get to the lavatory in time.'

### Who?
It's a disease that strikes young adults in their prime — and women more than men.

SOURCE: Institute of Neurology.

## 60,000
## have Parkinsons' disease
## (UK)

This is the commonest of involuntary movement disorders affecting one person in 1,000 and one in a 100 of the over-75s. Some progress has been made in understanding and treating Parkinson's disease. The causes include a depletion of the neurotransmitter, dopamine. Patients given L-dopa can improve considerably for a time, but in the end, perhaps after several years of treatment, the abnormal involuntary movements return along with various side effects such as visual pseudo hallucinations.

SOURCE: Institute of Neurology.

# 6,000,000
# care for disabled or elderly relations or friends at home

A recent survey by the Office of Population Censuses and Surveys has put the real figure of those who look after both disabled and elderly relatives at home at around 6,000,000 — or about **one adult in eight**. Such care can impose an extreme strain and even be a full-time job, preventing the carer from working or pursuing a career. The Family Policy Studies Centre argues that carers represent a major, underpublicised cause, comparable to the issue of childcare. Many carers need help and relief — at the same time as institutional facilities are being cut back.

## Who?

**M/F.**  2,500,000 men, and 3,500,000 women look after the elderly and disabled at home. The women are predominantly middle-aged and older, who are often putting in this work over and above any time they may spend or have spent looking after husband and children.

## Where?
1,700,000 people look after someone in the same household.

## How long?
Over 1,000,000 people spend 20 hours a week or more on care. Nearly 1,200,000 people have looked after the same person for over 10 years.

## Case study
Freddy and Pam Clifford, both in their seventies, look after their daughter, Gay, 45, who was once a successful academic. Gay recently had a massive brain haemorrhage, which virtually destroyed her memory and left her mentally disabled. 'Most of the time she sits and reads — she can read all sorts of things, but she has no idea what she's read. No idea what she's seen on TV,' says Pam. 'I don't suppose she'd ever go to bed unless someone told her to. One of the ghastly things is: nobody seems to understand the strain. You can never relax; we are never free.'

Source: Sunday Times, 25.9.88.

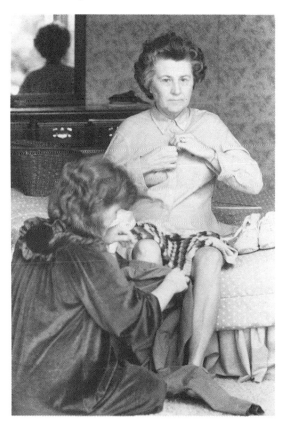

SOURCES: survey, H. Green, Informal Carers, OPCS (General Household Survey 1985 — GHS No. 15 Supplement A).

# MENTAL HANDICAP

**Hospital for people with mental handicaps, Ely**

## 1,000,000 have mental handicaps

About 2-3% of the population (1 to 1.5 million) people) have intellectual abilities low enough that they need support from social services at some time in their lives. Usually, that means they have an IQ of less than 70, although IQ is only a rough guide, and individuals have different strengths and weaknesses. Unlike mental illness, mental handicap cannot at present be cured because it is the result of physical damage to, or malformation of, the brain.

### Who?

**Mild difficulties (IQ 50-69).**   It is estimated that there are about 1 million such people. Most live independently in the community. Only a small percentage are dealt with by social services authorities.

**Severely handicapped (IQ below 49).**   It is estimated that there are about 160,000 such people in the UK, of whom 60,000 are children. Four out of five children and two out of five adults live with their families.

### In hospital

On average, in 1986, people with mental handicaps occupied 42,500 beds in hospitals and special units. There were 37,200 out-patient attendances in the same year.

**How long?**   Most patients in mental handicap hospitals and units are long-term residents. 82% in England in 1985 had been there for over five years. Only 7% had been there less than one year.

### Causes

Damage to the nervous system is detectable in about two-thirds of people with mental handicaps. There are many possible causes:
- chromosomal and genetic abnormalities;
- infections (e.g. flu and rubella);
- trauma (injury) (e.g. injury during birth), baby battering, accidents;
- socio-economic factors (e.g. malnutrition).

### Trends

People with mental handicaps, like the mentally ill, have been steadily pushed out into the community. Daily occupied beds fell by 35% between 1971 and 1986, while out-patient attendances were up 250%.

SOURCES: Mencap; Social Trends 1988.

# MENTAL HANDICAP

Down's syndrome is the commonest cause of institutionalisation for mental handicaps. Many sufferers have problems with speech and language. Some have more severe difficulties with basic functions like walking and going to the toilet.

Most people with Down's syndrome, provided they have help early on, can be successfully integrated into community life. An increasing number are now finding jobs.

## Causes
In 1959, it was first explained that Down's syndrome sufferers have 47 as distinct from the usual 46 chromosomes. Scientists are still trying to identify the individual or separate groups of genes responsible for conditions such as heart defects, blood disorders and mental retardation which are associated with Down's syndrome.

**Mothers.** The risk of having a Down's syndrome baby rises with age to one in 350 for mothers aged 35, and one in 45 for those over 45.

SOURCE: Down's Syndrome Association.

## 900
## babies born with Down's syndrome (UK, 1986)

---

## 80,000
## affected by autism (UK)

Autism is a profound life-long mental handicap, which is believed to be the result of organic brain damage rather than emotional trauma. It affects the whole process of communication. Autistic people have great difficulty interpreting and responding to other people's signals, as well as problems in learning. There is a wide spectrum of autistic conditions, ranging from profound severity to subtle problems of understanding in people of otherwise normal intelligence.

Of the approximately 80,000 sufferers, about a quarter will have classic autism, and the rest will have closely related conditions. All need similar services.

## Who?

**M/F.** It affects four times as many males as females.

## Prognosis
Out of every 100 autistic children, five to 10 will become independent as adults, 25 to 30 will make good progress but still need support and supervision. The rest will remain severely handicapped and dependent.

SOURCE: National Autistic Society.

# LONG-TERM SICKNESS

## 938,000
## had been claiming sickness/invalidity benefit for over six months (UK, 1986)

The numbers of long-term sick, i.e. those claiming sickness and invalidity benefit for over six months, are alarming — because they are not only so large, but rising steadily. Invalidity benefit, introduced in September 1971, replaces sickness benefit if incapacity continues after 168 days in any period of interruption of employment.

## Who?

**M/F.**   727,000 men and 211,000 women had been claiming for over six months.

**Age.**   Not all were older — 386,000 men and 196,000 women among the long-term sick were under 60. 340,000 men and 15,000 women were 60 and over.

## Trends

To judge by benefits, the numbers of long-term sick almost exactly doubled between 1976 and 1986, from a low of 468,000 in 1976. The trends have been steadily upwards, although care has to be taken in analysing them, due to modifications in diagnostic practice — mental disorders, for example, have probably increased in part due to greater public 'acceptability' of psychiatric ill-health.

## In hospital

These were the major diseases among those treated in NHS hospitals in Great Britain in 1986, by number of diagnoses:

| | |
|---|---|
| 1. Digestive system | 616,900 |
| 2. Respiratory system | 550,100 |
| 3. Cancers | 482,900 |
| 4. Heart (including rheumatic fever, hypertensive disease) | 417,200 |
| 5. Musculo-skeletal system | 334,200 |
| 6. Cerebrovascular disease | 298,500 |
| 7. Fractures, dislocations and sprains | 243,900 |
| 8. Complications of pregnancy, childbirth | 162,700 |
| 9. Diseases of urinary system | 126,000 |
| 10. Diseases of nervous system | 125,100 |

Source: Annual Abstract of Statistics 1988.

## 'I've a long-standing illness.'

**33% of the population of Great Britain in 1986 reported that they have a long-standing illness** according to the General Household Survey. This, it has to be stressed, is self-reported illness, but it is still an interesting reflection of human frailty.

Sources: General Household Survey 1986; Regional Trends 1988)

# LONG-TERM SICKNESS

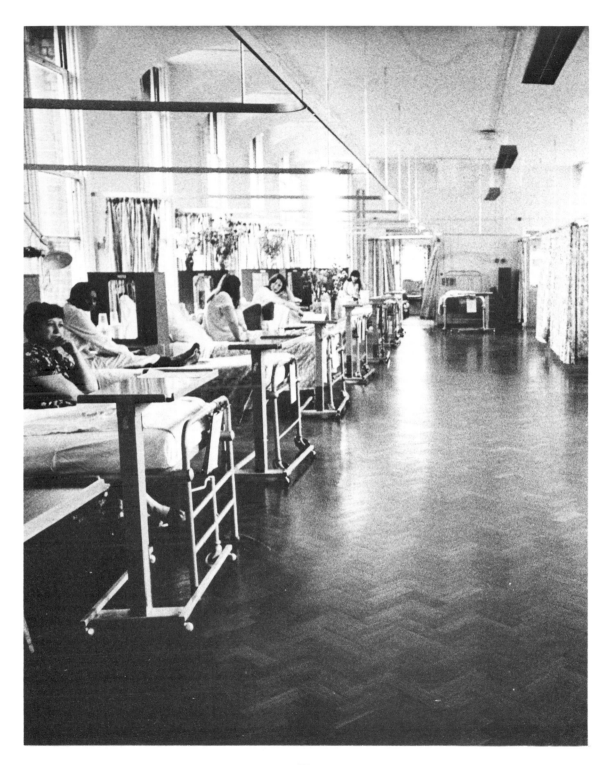

# DISEASES

## RHEUMATOID ARTHRITIS:
## 300,000 sufferers

Nearly all of us will eventually fall victim to one of the various arthritic and rheumatic diseases one day; they currently affect about a third of the population (mostly over the age of 65 and are the single major cause of disability in the UK. About 8 million seek some form of medical treatment each year, with about 1.5 million attending a hospital for the first time, referred by their doctor.

There are 200 different forms of arthritis of which only gout can be cured — although medical researchers are hopeful of ultimately finding cures. The other types of arthritis respond to different forms of treatment.

**Rheumatoid arthritis** is the commonest type of inflammatory arthritis found in Britain affecting about 2 million people — predominantly women (3:1), usually aged between 30 and 50. 300,000 need constant assessment and treatment.

**Osteoarthritis** affects about 5-6 million people leaving 200,000 housebound.

**Ankylosing spondilitis** affects the spine, ultimately preventing people from straightening, and thus impairing lung function. It affects 70,000 people.

### Who?
Arthritis mainly affects the aged — two out of three people over 65. But it affects the young too — around 12,000 children, including babies, and as many as one in 10 of 17-40-year-olds.

### Cost
About 80 million working days are lost each year in the UK through arthritis — less than 2 million were lost through industrial action in 1986 — with a loss of economic productivity estimated in excess of £1 billion.

SOURCES: Arthritis and Rheumatism Council for Research; The 35 Group of Arthritis Care.

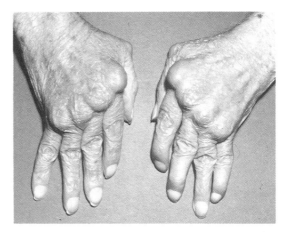

**Severe rheumatoid arthritis**

## PEPTIC ULCERS:
## 1,000,000 sufferers

Peptic ulcers are small holes occurring in the stomach (gastric ulcers) or duodenum (duodenal ulcers), when the lining tissue is worn down by acid and enzyme secretions. 10% of us can expect to have an ulcer in our lifetime. Since the mid-1970s the drugs Tagamet and Zantac have considerably improved treatment by reducing acid secretion, but patients still tend to have recurrent bouts of ulcers. There is still much to discover about the causes.

# DISEASES

## DIABETES:
## 750,000 sufferers

It is estimated that a further 250,000 undiagnosed people suffer from diabetes, making up about 2% of the UK population.

### Who?
There are 18,000 diabetics under 20. The rate has mysteriously doubled since 1968, from 10 per 10,000 to 20 per 10,000, mainly in the two richest socio-economic groups and particularly in rural areas. 60,000 new cases are diagnosed each year, over 3,000 among people under the age of 20.

### Causes
About 90% of diabetes is related to overweight and obesity and is potentially preventable.

Source: 'Insulin-dependent?', The Lancet, 12 October 1985: 809-810.

### Effects

**Death.** **20,000 people of all ages die prematurely each year as a result of diabetes**. Sufferers are particularly at risk of heart disease, strokes and kidney failure.

**Blindness.** One in six of the people under the age of 65 registered blind each year go blind because of diabetes. Diabetes can also lead to heart disease, kidney damage and gangrene.

SOURCE: British Diabetic Association

## BACK PAIN:
## 2,000,000 sufferers

Of the 2,000,000 sufferers who go to their GPs with back pain each year, 400,000 a year are referred to hospital.

### Who?
Most at risk are 45-65-year-olds — 6.8% of men and 6.2% of women aged 45-65 consult a GP at least once a year for back pain. Also at risk are tall, overweight people, and those who do work that involves a lot of lifting and twisting.

### Recovery
70% get better within one month, 90% within three months, but 30% (600,000) have a recurrence within a year.

### Cost
33 million working days are lost each year because of back pain, accounting for nearly 10% of all loss of work due to ill health. Medications for back pain are calculated by the Office of Health Economics to cost around £39 million a year.

SOURCES: Professor Malcolm Jayson, Back Pain: The Facts; Back Pain Association.

# DISEASES

## HEART DISEASE:
## 800,000 sufferers

Not only is heart disease the Number One killer, but it also causes suffering for some 2,000,000 people. Over 800,000 consult their GPs each year. 21% of all absenteeism from work among men is caused by heart disease. A National Audit Office report, released in February 1989, found that ministerial departments' reponses to the disease have been slow and unco-ordinated

compared with efforts against AIDS and drug abuse.

### Cost
The cost to the NHS of treating heart disease is estimated at about £390 million. The cost to industry of the disease, according to Patrick Nicholl, the Junior Minister for Employment, speaking on 19 April 1989, is about £1.5 billion a year.

SOURCES: Office of Health Economics; British Heart Foundation.

---

## SEXUALLY TRANSMITTED DISEASES:
## 704,000 new cases (UK, 1986)

As sexual liberation has increased, so has sexual disease. New cases of sexual diseases at hospital clinics have more than doubled over the last 15 years. But apart from the looming spectre of AIDS the main increase has been in relatively harmless, non-specific genital infections.

### Main diseases
The numbers of new cases at NHS hospital clinics in 1986 were :

| | |
|---|---|
| Syphilis | 3,000 |
| Gonorrhea | 46,000 |
| Herpes simplex | 20,000 |
| Non-specific genital infection | 175,000 |

There were also over 300,000 'other conditions requiring treatment', including such things as warts, pubic lice, and 'thrush', and 154,000 not requiring treatment.

### Who?

**M/F.** Men suffered more from sexual disease with a total of 386,000 new cases against 318,000 for women. They had significantly more gonorrhea (28,000 cases against women's 18,000), and non-specific genital infection (119,000 cases against 56,000).

### Trends
Sexual disease more than doubled between 1971 (338,000 new cases in NHS clinics) and 1986 (704,000 new cases in NHS clinics). While non-specific genital infection and herpes have increased significantly, gonorrhea has gone down (from 63,000 cases), and syphilis has remained constant and relatively negligible.

SOURCE: Social Trends 1988.

# OVERWEIGHT

## 12,500,000 (35% of GB population aged 16-64) were overweight (1980)

While some peoples in the world starve, the British overeat — at any rate, many of us do. Overweight and obesity are particularly concentrated among the over-40s. The answer may lie in more physical exercise and a less sedentary life for the middle-aged.

> **Over 50% of men between 40 and 64 are overweight.**

## Overweight/obese?

One can only make crude estimates of how many obese people there are within any population. The figure of 12,500,000 is based on the Body Mass Index which compares people's weight and height. Examples of both categories are as follows:

| Height | 'Overweight' | 'Obese' |
|--------|-------------|---------|
| 5'6" | 11 stone, 3lb | 13 stone, 6lb |
| 5'9" | 12 stone, 4lb | 14 stone, 11lb |
| 6' | 13 stone, 6lb | 16 stone, 2lb |

## Who?

**M/F.** More men are overweight — 39% of all men aged 16-64, against only 32% for women.

**Age.** Being overweight increases steadily with age. Only about 12% of 16-19-year-olds are overweight. But 40% of men aged 30-39 are overweight, and for men aged 40-64, it's a fairly constant figure of about 50%. The proportion of overweight women rises more steadily, from less than 40% around the age 40, to over 50% around 60-64.

## Effects

A high fat, low fibre diet is strongly associated with heart disease — the foremost killer in this country. Saturated fatty acids can increase the concentration of cholesterol in the blood, which is strongly linked to heart problems. Obesity also increases the risk of diabetes.

> **Fatism and sizeism**
> On 20 March 1989, the first Fat Women's Conference was held in London. Politician Mandy Mudd said: 'Fat people have been stereotyped as being lazy and unhealthy. We want to change the way society treats them, and to help fat people feel better about themselves . . . I don't find my own fatness a problem, but I find other people's attitude to it a problem.'

## Trends

Comparisons with national surveys conducted since the 1930s show a steady trend towards increasing fatness. On the other hand, more recently there has been a steady, if slow, improvement in the nation's diet and health. Overall, our fat intake has fallen about 10% since 1959. In 1987, for example, we ate much fewer dairy products than in 1971 — 37% fewer eggs, 21% less milk and cream, and 65% less butter. And our tooth was not so sweet — we ate 23% fewer cakes and biscuits, and a staggering 59% less sugar.

On the positive side, we're eating more fruit and vegetables and vegetarianism is on the rise. With the current emphasis on healthy living these trends seem likely to continue.

SOURCES: Heights and Weights of Adults in Great Britain, Office of Population Censuses and Surveys 1984; Social Trends 1989.

# MENTAL ILLNESS

## 82,500
## — average hospital population (UK, 1986)
## 256,500 new outpatients

The mentally ill are increasingly being treated in the community rather than in hospital. The number of hospital beds for them has been sharply cut back over the last two decades, and at least 55 out of 178 large psychiatric hospitals are involved in closure plans according to a June 1988 announcement in the Commons, and still more according to other sources.

Some cuts have been motivated by idealistic as well as economic considerations. In the sixties, life within institutions came to be seen as itself disabling, life within the community as liberating and helping to restore self-respect.

But the mentally ill sent back into the community still need care, and many have not been getting it. Some have ended up lonely and isolated, in hostels, boarding houses or bedsits. Others have simply become homeless — up to 50% of the destitute and homeless have severe mental health problems. Others have returned to families unable to cope.

'**We are very seriously worried about the way the seriously mentally ill are being tossed out on to the street with little or no follow-up, back-up or proper supervision. It is one of the most appalling things happening in Britain today.**' Judy Weleminsky, Director of the National Schizophrenic Fellowship.

While the question of *where* the mentally ill should be treated occupies much attention, all the unsolved problems of *how* they should be treated remain. One of the most significant facts about psychiatric practice today is that over 70% of admissions to psychiatric hospitals in 1986 were re-admissions.

Sources: On the State of the Public Health 1987.

**Powick Hospital, Worcestershire**

# MENTAL ILLNESS

## Which illnesses?

In 1986, for the 197,251 people admitted to psychiatric hospital in England, the major diagnoses were:

| | |
|---|---|
| 1. Depressive disorders | 35,209 |
| 2. Schizophrenia, paranoia | 29,419 |
| 3. Affective psychoses | 24,633 |
| 4. Senile and presenile dementia | 20,858 |
| 5. Alcohol dependent syndrome | 11,809 |

Dementia is the one significant growth area with cases more than doubling since 1971 as the older population has increased.

Source: Health and Personal Social Services Statistics 1986.

## How long?

34% of resident patients in mental illness hospitals and units in England in 1985 had been there for over five years, 43% for under one year.

Source: Social Trends 1988.

---

## The nation's mental health

Studies have shown a high level of mental and emotional stress in the community. **250 people out of 1,000 will experience psychiatric symptoms at any one time**, of whom 230 will consult a GP; 140 will be treated, usually with psychotropic drugs; 17 will be referred to an out-patient psychiatric clinic; and six will be admitted to psychiatric hospital.

Source: Review of Community Care, MIND July 1987.

---

## Costs

Mental illness and mental handicap account for 20% of NHS costs, according to the Economic Adviser's Office at the DHSS, and 14% of days off work on certified sickness. (The last figure is probably a considerable underestimate since mental illness does not always appear on sickness certificates.)

Source: On the State of the Nation's Health 1987.

## Local authority care

24 local authorities still have no day care at all for people with mental illness. The Social Services Select Committee has called this an appalling inadequacy. The number of community psychiatric nurses rose by 900 in the four years 1980-84 but still only stood at 2,200 in 1984.

## Trends

Mental illness hospitals and units in England have been admitting somewhat more people — up from 175,000 in 1975, to 197,000 in 1986. But they're turning people out faster. Their average patient population has fallen from 131,900 in 1971 to 82,500 in 1986. Beds were cut by 25,000 in the decade to 1987, while only 4,000 new residential places were set up in the community. The trend will continue, with around 60 psychiatric hospitals set to close over the next 10 years, and a consequent exodus of 20,000 people who will require care and support in the community.

SOURCES: Health and Personal Social Services Statistics 1986; Social Trends 1988; Report to Sir Roy Griffiths, Review of Community Care, MIND July 1987.

# MENTAL ILLNESS

## 250,000 schizophrenics

Roughly 15% of all admissions to mental illness hospitals in England in 1986 (29,419) were for schizophrenia. For most of these — around 87% — this was not their first time. Schizophrenia is an illness which leaves many permanently scarred, and we still have much to understand about its causes.

The figure of 250,000 schizophrenics altogether is an estimate of all those who have been *diagnosed*, and includes the 20% or so who have fully recovered, as well as those who are ill now or have residual symptoms, and those who may have a relapse in the future.

### Prevalence
Estimates vary, but about onr in 100 will develop schizophrenia at some stage in their life.

### Symptoms include:
- loss of energy, excessive sleeping, self-neglect, hiding away from people;
- hearing 'voices';
- thinking others are against you, when they are not;
- confused, muddled thinking and speech.

### When?
The age of first onset is 24 on average for men and 30 for women.

### Recovery
20% of people first admitted with a diagnosis of schizophrenia make a complete recovery. But over half are left with significant residual symptoms and seriously impaired social functioning, which needs long-term treatment and care. They are 11 times more likely to commit suicide than the general population. Up to one in 10 sufferers kill themselves.

Sources: National Schizophrenia Fellowship; On the State of the Public Health 1987.

---

## 10% of the over-65s suffer from senile dementia

Senile dementia is an increasingly serious problem, due to the rapidly increasing *numbers* of elderly people. Research suggests that some 20% of people over 80 are likely to suffer from a significant degree of dementia. It involves loss of mental powers, including impaired recall and difficulty in retaining new knowledge. Around 80% of cases are due to Alzheimer's disease, in which brain tissue shrinks and nerve fibres become distorted, leading in the most advanced stage to complete mental and physical deterioration. Almost everything, even the difference between day and night, may be forgotten.

Some progress has been made in understanding dementia — an abnormal protein has been found in Alzheimer brains — but the real causes are still not known.

### Trends
The rate of admission to mental hospitals for dementia, for those 75 and over, has risen from 284 per 100,000 in 1976 to 488 per 100,000 in 1986.

Source: Mental Health Enquiry, DHSS.

SOURCE: Institute of Neurology.

# MENTAL ILLNESS

**West Park Mental Hospital, Epsom**

## 24,633
## admitted to hospital with affective psychoses (England, 1986)

## One person in 200 suffers from manic depression

Affective psychoses, which include manic depression, accounted for roughly 12% of all admissions to mental hospital in England in 1986. Although less seriously damaging to the personality than schizophrenia, they can cause great distress to both sufferers and their families — and victims are much more likely to kill themselves than schizophrenics. Some estimates place the rate of manic depressives in the population as high as one in a 100.

### Who?

**M/F.** Women outnumber men manic depressives by about two to one.

**Age.** The first onset of manic depression is not usually before 14, but can then occur any time onwards.

### Rate
There are some 370 hospital admissions per 100,000 of the population per year in the UK. Only 3% of these are first time admissions.

SOURCES: Health and Personal Social Services Statistics; Manic Depression Fellowship.

# SMOKING

## 14,000,000 smokers (GB) 100,000 smoking-related deaths every year

Smokers are now a minority among all social classes, and smoking has been declining among most groups throughout the decade. The general trend though seems to be downwards. And it is

encouraging to see how many people have already kicked the habit.

But 14,000,000 adult smokers, even if they only form a third of the population, is a huge number. Smoking remains 'the single most important preventable cause of premature death and sickness in Britain, being responsible for the shortening of the lives of about 100,000 Britons each year'.

SOURCE: On the State of the Public Health 1987.

## Who?

**M/F.**  In 1986, 35% of men and 31% of women were smokers, according to ASH. Markedly more men than women over 60 smoke, but there are no differences between the sexes among 16-19-year-olds, where 30% of each sex smoke.

Source: Cigarette Smoking: 1972 to 1986, OPCS Monitor SS 88/1 9/2/88.

**Class.**  More manual and unskilled workers smoke. In 1986, 43% of unskilled manual men smoked, compared to 18% of professional men. (In 1972 the corresponding figures were 64% and 33%.)

Source: General Household Survey 1986.

**Schoolchildren.**  Surveys have shown that approximately 50% of schoolchildren have tried cigarettes by the age of 13, and roughly 20% are regular smokers by the age of 15.

## How many?

Britons smoked almost 95 billion cigarettes in 1986, an average consumption for smokers of 115 cigarettes a week for men, and 96 cigarettes a week for women.

## Deaths and disease

It is estimated that 100,000 people in the UK are killed by smoking each year. Most die from the three main diseases associated with cigarette smoking:

- lung cancer,
- chronic obstructive lung disease/(bronchitis and emphysema), and
- coronary heart disease.

90% of deaths from the first two are estimated to be smoking-related, and 20% of deaths from CHD.

Research has also shown a connection between cervical cancer and smoking. About 70% of women found to have pre-cancerous cervical abnormalities are smokers.

Source: Health or Smoking? (Report of the Royal College of Physicians) 1983; Imperial Cancer Research Fund.

## Costs

Smoking-related diseases cost the National Health Service an estimated £500 million a year.

Source: Social Trends 1989.

---

**10,000,000 people in Britain have given up smoking.**

---

## International comparison

Only 29% of Americans now smoke. **'The ashtray is following the spitoon into oblivion.'** Dr Everett Koop, USA Surgeon General.

## Trends

Smoking has steadily declined since the early 1970s, both in terms of numbers of smokers and sales of cigarettes. Smokers became a minority of the adult population in 1976, and a minority in every socio-economic group in 1982. Sales of packeted cigarettes fell by over 25% between 1976 and 1986.

But a warning for the future: Central Statistical Office figures for January-September 1988 actually show a 2.2% increase in smoking over the same period in 1987. Anti-smoking campaigners believe this is due to the fall in real terms of the cost of cigarettes and were extremely disappointed that taxes were not raised in the budget of March 1989.

Source: ASH (Action on Smoking and Health).

# DRINKING

## 700,000
## alcoholics (UK)

Drugs like heroin, cannabis and, recently, 'crack' and 'ecstasy', may attract more attention, but alcohol abuse is far and away the gravest addiction problem in the UK. About 2% of the adult population is seriously dependent on alcohol — 700,000 people, according to the Office of Health and Economics (and 750,000, according to ACCEPT, Addictions Community Centres for Education, Prevention and Treatment). Another 650,000 people have a definite drinking problem.

## 3,000,000
## heavy drinkers (UK)

About 8% of the total adult population are heavy drinkers, i.e. exceed the safe levels recommended by the royal medical colleges of 21 units of alcohol a week for men and 14 units for women. [1 unit equals half a pint of beer, or a single shot of spirits, or one glass of wine.]

A variety of bodies concerned to prevent alcoholic abuse are pressing for increased taxes on alcohol, restrictions on drink advertising, and improved public education and information.

Source: Office of Health Economics.

## Who?

**M/F.** Men drink much more than women — 20% are heavy drinkers compared with only 2% of women, (although the latter are on the increase). Heaviest of all are men aged 18-24 and 25-44, of whom 34% and 27% respectively exceed the safe limit.

Source: General Household Survey 1985

**Schoolchildren.** The young are starting to drink sooner — on average, for both boys and girls, between 12 and 14. 52% of 15-year-old boys and 37% of 15-year-old girls drink at least weekly.

Source: OPCS Adolescent Drinking Survey 1984.

**Yuppies** Ray Hatter of the Alcohol Advisory Service estimates that about 40,000 of the 300,000 people working in the City — a higher proportion than the national average — have an alcohol problem due to a combination of high incomes and high stress jobs.

## Non-drinkers
7% of men and 13% of women classified themselves as abstainers in 1984.

Source: General Household Survey

# DRINKING

## How much?

**Drinks per year.** In a year, the average Briton (18 and over) drinks:

| | |
|---|---|
| Beer (pints) | 250 |
| Table wine — glasses (1/6 bottle) | 93 |
| Sherry — glasses (1/14 bottle) | 19 |
| Port — glasses (1/14 bottle) | 5 |
| Whisky — tots (1/32 bottle) | 111 |
| Gin — tots (1/32 bottle) | 32 |

Source: Economist Diary 1988, based on 1986 figures.

**Spending per year.** In 1986, we spent £16.5 billion on alcohol, more than on clothing, fuel, or holidays — some 7% of all consumer expenditure.

Source: Central Statistical Office.

**Media.** Drink appears or is mentioned on over half of all evening TV programmes, according to a 1988 survey. Of 394 programmes watched, 51% showed people drinking, mentioned drink or contained drink ads. Only one showed someone refusing a drink.

Source: National Viewers' and Listeners' Association survey, 23.11.88.

**Advertising.** Over £200 million a year is spent on drink advertising.

Source: Action on Alcohol Abuse.

## Consequences

**Accidents.** Drinking and driving leads to:

- 20% of road deaths in Britain — over 1,000 a year
- 33% of driver and motorcycle rider deaths
- 10% of all accidents involving injuries

Source: Transport and Road Research Laboratory.

**Crime.** A variety of studies have shown that alcohol abuse is a significant factor in crime, connecting it with over 50% of murders, rapes, violent offences, assaults, and criminal damage.

Sources: Alcohol Concern, Action on Alcohol Abuse.

**Divorce.** One-third of divorce petitions cite alcohol as a contributing factor.

Source: Don W. Steele, 'Alcohol', in Long Range Planning, vol. 20, No. 5 pp86-90, 1987.

**Deaths.** Alcohol lies at the root of between 25,000 and 40,000 deaths every year and causes more than an estimated 80% of deaths from chronic liver disease. According to the Royal College of General Practitioners, is also accounts for:
40% of deaths through injuries and poisonings
12% of deaths from digestive diseases
11% of deaths through respiratory disease
12% of deaths through heart disease
4% of deaths through malignant growths, including cancers.

Source: Keep Alcohol Safeguards.

## Trends

The fashion for healthier living may have affected drinking in the eighties. A variety of figures and surveys show a long, slow decline in heavy drinking and associated convictions for drunkenness and drunken driving. But, while per capita consumption may have decreased, total alcohol consumption has almost doubled over the last 30 years and, in 1987, increased again. So too did the number of drink offences. As anti-alcohol organisations are quick to point out, it is still too soon to talk of a definite trend.

SOURCES: Alcohol Concern; Action on Alcohol Abuse.

# DRUGS

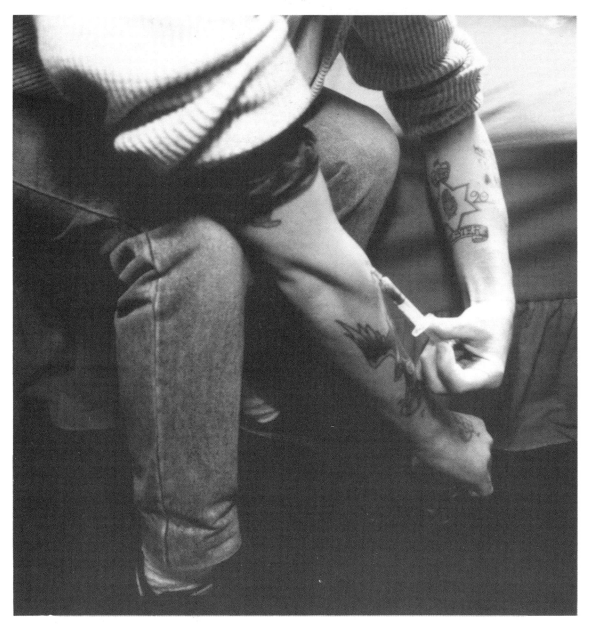

## 50,000–100,000 heroin addicts (UK)

Assessing the number of heroin addicts and misusers of other illicit drugs is notoriously difficult. The above figure is based on an estimate that for every registered heroin addict, there are six to 10 more who are not known. There were 10,398 registered drug addicts in the UK in 1987, receiving notified drugs in treatment. About 90% of registered addicts are heroin users.

Drug addiction has increased substantially in the 1980s, and the government campaigns against heroin were a recognition of how serious the problem has become. Quite recently, there have been reports that cocaine and 'crack' are replacing heroin as the Number One drugs. Seizures of cocaine at British ports in 1988 outweighed and outnumbered seizures of heroin for the first time.

Another major problem arising from drug addiction is the spread of AIDS through drug users sharing needles.

## Who?

**Past history.** In 1987, 4,593 new addicts were registered for the first time, along with 3,100 former addicts who had started re-using drugs. **In 1988, the number of new addicts rose again by over 14% to a record 8,800**.

**M/F.** 71% of new addicts in 1988 were men, and 29% were women.

**Age.** The average age of new addicts in 1988 was 26. The biggest increase in new addicts then was among those aged 25-29.

**Schoolchildren.** A recent survey of 18,000 secondary schoolchildren showed that among 15-year-olds, roughly one in five pupils had been offered drugs — 19% of boys and 12% of girls had been offered cannabis, and half of these had tried it. Only 4% of boys and 2% of girls had been offered heroin, and only a quarter of these had tried it.

Source: John Balding, Young People in 1987, Exeter University, November 1988.

## Consequences

**Drug convictions.** 23,200 people were found guilty of drug offences in England and Wales in 1987.

Source: Criminal Statistics England and Wales 1987.

**Prison.** 1,337 addicts were admitted to penal institutions in 1987.

**Mental hospital.** In 1985, 4,384 people were admitted to mental hospitals with a drug-related diagnosis — 2,862 men and 1,522 women.

Source: DHSS; Welsh Office.

**AIDS.** As a recent government advertising campaign has emphasised, there is a considerable danger of addicts who share needles passing on AIDS. Between half and two-thirds of addicts are injecting drugs, according to a Home Office estimate in 1989.

**Deaths.** In 1987, there were 399 drug-related deaths, up considerably from 336 in 1986, and sharply from 192 in 1978.

Source: Drugs Inspectorate, DHSS.

## Trends

There has been an almost continuous increase in drug addiction since the early 1970s, according to all indicators. Admissions to mental hospital have doubled since 1971. Drug convictions almost doubled in five years, between 1979 and 1984. And notified addicts have increased *sevenfold* from 1,405 in 1973.

Sources: Social Trends 1989; Home Office.

# SOLVENT ABUSE

## 80
## deaths from solvent abuse
## (UK, 1986)

Solvents (including glue and other volatile solvents) are another underpublicised form of addiction. More pupils have tried solvents, or use them daily, than any other drug, according to the British Journal of Addiction. Other sources agree that solvents are much more widely used than heroin, but much less so than cannabis. The average age at which solvents were first used was under 13. Solvent abuse is rising particularly among girls.

Source: Re-Solv 1988.

### How?
51 of the 80 solvent-related deaths were due to direct toxic effects, 11 to inhalation of vomit, three to plastic bags stuck over the head, and another 15 to trauma.

### Regions
One local study suggested that as many as 20-25% of 13—15-year-old boys in Glasgow had misused solvents.

Source: Surveys and Statistics on Drug-taking in Britain, ISDD, 1984.

### Trends
Deaths have risen from 31 in 1980, to 72 in 1983 to 80 in 1986.

Sources: Institute for the Study of Drug Dependence (ISDD); St George's Hospital Medical School, 1987; Children in Danger, 1989; National Children's Home.

# TRANQUILLISERS

## 200,000–500,000 addicts

Tranquillisers are a far more widespread addiction problem than heavy drugs, although it's difficult to establish the exact extent. Estimates vary because they are based on small-scale studies, but there seems to be agreement that the number of addicts lies in the hundreds of thousands.

Tranquillisers are among the most commonly prescribed drugs in the western world. While they can be useful in dealing with a specific trauma for a few days, their effects tend to wear off after four months, when they often become addictive. Some long-term users can give them up without any trouble. Many have very painful withdrawal symptoms — which are thought to last for a month for every year on tranquillisers.

A MORI poll in February 1984, commissioned by That's Life!, showed that over **3,500,000 people had taken tranquillisers for longer than four and a half months**.

Sources: ed. A. Herxheimer, 'Some problems with benzodiazepines', Drug & Therapeutics Bulletin, vol. 23, 21-23, 1985; H. Ashton, 'Dangers and medico-legal aspects of benzodiazepines', Journal of Medical Defence Union, Summer 1987; That's Life! survey on Tranquillisers, BBC 1985.

## Who?

**All users.**   The MORI poll also found that 10,000,000 people — 23% of the adult population — had taken tranquillisers at some time.

**M/F.**   Tranquillisers are prescribed twice as often for women as men. Those at greatest risk of abnormal depression are young to middle-aged working-class women.

Sources: MIND; ed. Alwyn Smith and Bobbie Jacobson, The Nation's Health 1988.

## Which drugs?

The main tranquillisers used nowadays are the benzodiazepines, including Valium, Ativan, Librium, Mogadon and Dalmane, which, as distinct from barbiturates, are non-toxic.

## Cost

11,238,000 tranquilliser prescriptions were handed out in England alone in 1986 at a cost of £14,416,000.

SOURCE: Health and Personal Social Services Statistics 1988.

# TV VIEWING

## The average Briton watches 25 hours of TV every week

Is TV viewing an unhealthy addiction or a healthy quest for information? Or a little of both? Whatever the truth, we spend about a seventh of our lives in front of the TV set.

## Who?

**Class.** Lower socio-economic groups watch much more per week. In January to March 1987, ABs watched 20¾ hours every week, while DEs watched 35 hours. But there is surprisingly little overall difference in what the groups watch.

**Age.** The elderly watch *much more* TV — 42 hours a week against 16½ hours a week by 16—24-year-olds. Schoolchildren watch less TV than the average. Nevertheless, according to a recent Exeter University survey, about **50% of schoolchildren spend more time in front of a TV than a teacher each year**. Among 11-year-olds, for example, 41% of boys and 35% of girls watch TV more than 21 hours a week. At 14 the figures start to drop.

Source: survey, John Balding, Young People in 1987, Exeter University 1988.

## When?

Not surprisingly, much more TV is watched in winter months. Males watched only 21 hours a week in July-September 1986 and females only 24 hours.

## What?

The majority of viewers do *not* spend nearly all their time watching pap. All social groups spend roughly a quarter of their time on Information and News, and 40% viewing light entertainment and light drama.

| | % of time spent viewing by: | |
| --- | --- | --- |
| | ABC1* | C2DE* |
| Light entertainment | 16% | 15% |
| Light drama | 24% | 26% |
| Information | 18% | 17% |
| News | 10% | 9% |
| Sport | 9% | 9% |
| Films | 11% | 12% |

*the top and bottom three socio-economic groups, respectively

Source: Patrick Barwise and Andrew Ehrenberg, Television and its Audience 1989.

## Licence evasion

About 1.4 million households (roughly one in 14), were estimated to be evading licence fees in September 1987. 162,000 people were actually convicted for TV licence evasion, as against 163,000 the previous year.

> One in three prefer to watch TV than make love — 44% of women and 22% of men — according to a Gallup poll of couples aged 18 to 60, for TV makes Hinari.

SOURCES: Broadcasting Audience Research Board; Audits of Great Britain; Social Trends 1988.

## The UK spent £166 a head on gambling in 1986

Gamblers Anonymous estimates that there are around 100,000 compulsive gamblers in Britain, suffering from an illness much like alcoholism. Such a figure is obviously very difficult to corroborate. Few figures are available apart from the overall spending on gambling activities. Some forms of gambling do seem to be on the decline. But others, particularly gaming machines, are on the increase.

### Which kinds?
Here is what the average adult (aged 18 years and over) laid out as stakes in 1986 on:

| | |
|---|---|
| Horse racing | £68 |
| Dog racing | £22 |
| Football pools | £12 |
| Bingo | £11 |
| Gaming machines | £20 |
| Gaming clubs | £33 |
| Total | £166 |

Source: Economist Diary 1988.

### Where?
In 1986, there were 10,407 betting offices, 1,186 bingo halls, 114 casinos, and 200,400 gaming machines in operation. 4,350,000 people attended greyhound meetings, and 3,958,000 went to horse races.

### Who?
Schoolchildren particularly use gaming machines. A major survey in 1988 by the National Housing and Town Planning Council of over 10,000 children found that **262,000 schoolchildren aged 13-16 (14% of the total), visited an amusement arcade and/or played gambling machines elsewhere at least once a week**.

For 3% of schoolchildren, the figure was four times a week or more. For another 43%, it was once a month. Many children spent a lot of money; 728,000 usually spent over £1 on a visit to an arcade, and 135,000 spent over £3. A significant proportion of these children, according to the Children's Society, take to crime to finance their gambling.

A Home Office survey published in July 1988 contradicted these findings, claiming that youngsters were spending very little on amusement arcades. But a later Exeter University survey tended to support the NHTPC, finding that one in three children had used slot machines in the last four weeks.

Sources: survey, Gambling Machines and Young People, National Housing and Town Planning Council, 1988; survey, John Balding, Young People in 1987, Exeter University, 1988.

### Trends
The number of people doing the pools and attending racing meetings has fallen in recent years. Greyhound attendances have halved from 8,800,000 in 1971. Bingo clubs are down from 1,775 in 1976. But the total number of gaming machines has increased by almost a quarter from 164,500 in 1976.

SOURCE: Social Trends 1988.

# INEQUALITY

## The wealthiest 5% own 25% of the nation's wealth
## The wealthiest 50% own 81%

The UK is one of the 33 European states which, in 1985, signed the World Health Organisation's European Targets for Health for All, the declared aim of which is that each country should reduce health inequalities by 25% by the year 2000. (As the Effects section below shows, inequalities of health accompany inequalities of income.) However, there is no sign of any serious programme to achieve that aim. And according to two reports reviewing government policy over the past 10 and 20 years, nor has there been a goal of abolishing child poverty in particular.

Sources: Alan Walker and Carol Walker (eds), The Growing Divide: A Social 'Audit 1979-87, Child Poverty Action Group, 1986; David Piachaud, Poor Children: A Tale of Two Decades, CPAG 1986.

---

### The richest 200

According to the Sunday Times, the richest 200 in Britain own:
- £38 billion of assets — equivalent to 8% of Britain's gross national product;
- 3.3 million acres (outside London) — about 7% of the total UK land mass.

These 200 include:
- a high percentage of nobility: 11 dukes, out of 25; six marquesses, out of 27; 14 earls, out of 145; and nine viscounts, out of 103;
- 55 Old Etonians.

**Only 43% made their fortunes for themselves — the rest represent old or inherited money**

---

## Distribution of wealth

According to estimates of marketable wealth in the UK in 1985 (including occupational and state pension rights) the wealthiest:

| | | |
|---|---|---|
| 1% | own | 11% of wealth; |
| 5% | own | 25%; |
| 10% | own | 35%; |
| 25% | own | 57%; |
| 50% | own | 81%. |

Total Marketable Wealth (without pensions): £863 billion

## Distribution of income

According to estimates of the share of total final income in the UK in 1986, by household group rather than by individuals, the:

| | | |
|---|---|---|
| Top 20% | earned | 41.7% of total income; |
| Top 40% | earned | 65.6%; |
| Bottom 40% | earned | 17.3%; |
| Bottom 20% | earned | 5.9%. |

## Trends

The richest have come to own less of total personal wealth since the 1970s. In 1971, for example, the top 1% owned 21% rather than 11% of wealth and the top 5% owned 37% rather than 25%. According to Social Trends, much of this was due to the decline in share values in the early 1970s.

On the other hand, high-earners are earning even higher percentages of total income. The top 20% only earned 37.9% of the total in 1976, compared to 41.7% in 1986, and the bottom 20% earned 7.4% compared to 5.9%.

SOURCE: Social Trends 1989.

## Effects of inequality and poverty

The publication of the Black Report on inequalities in health in 1980 seems to have stimulated a mass of subsequent research on the subject. As a result, it has been shown beyond doubt that poorer social classes have substantially worse health than richer classes.

## Deaths.
Poorer socio-economic groups are more likely to die at *every stage* of life.
- **Stillbirths:** In 1984 in England and Wales Class V unskilled manual workers had a rate of stillbirths *twice* that of Class I professionals, at over 8 per 1,000 total births compared with less than 4 in Class I.
- **Infant deaths:** In 1984 in England and Wales Class V workers had nearly *double* the infant death rate of Class I professionals, with roughly 13 infant deaths per 1,000 live births.
- **Men 20-64:** Class V workers in Great Britain in 1979-83 had well over *double* the Standard Mortality Ratio of Class I, with a Standard Mortality Ratio of over 150, compared with an SMR of under 70 in Class I.
- **Women 20-59:** Class V women in Great Britain, 1979-83, were also almost *twice* as likely to die as Class I women.
- **Men 65-74:** Even in retirement, men in Class V in Great Britain in 1976-81 were about *twice* as likely to die than men in occupational Class I.

## Health.
The general health of poorer socio-economic groups is much worse:
- **Long-standing illness:** Both men and women in Class V had more than *double* the rate of limiting long-standing illness of those in Class I in 1984. The differences were particularly marked in the middle-aged. About 10% of men aged 45-64 in Class I had a limiting long-standing illness, compared with about 40% in Class V, and for women 45-64 the comparable figures were under 10% in Class I against over 30% in Class V.
- **'Fair/poor health':** One survey showed 36% of men in Class V describing their health as fair or poor, against only 12% of men in Class I.

Source: B. Cox et al., Health and Lifestyle Survey, Preliminary Report, Health Promotion Research Trust 1987.

## Lifestyle.
Poorer socio-economic groups have a less healthy lifestyle — they drink more, smoke more, eat worse food. They are subject to considerably more stress as a result of poorer living and working conditions and greater income worries. It is not uncommon for poor people to forsake meals.
- **Smoking:** In 1984, 49% of unskilled manual men smoked, compared to 17% of professional men. (In 1972 the corresponding figures were 64% and 33%).
Source: General Household Survey.
- **Drinking:** In 1984, 26% of unskilled manual workers were classed as heavy drinkers, compared to 8% of professional men.
- **Diet:** The poorest 10% of households (Group D below) had a much poorer diet than the richest 10% (Group A) in 1984 in Great Britain:

**Consumption of staple foods (ounces per person per week)**

|  | D | A |
| --- | --- | --- |
| White bread | 26 | 12.3 |
| Sugar | 11.5 | 8 |
| Potatoes | 48.3 | 33.4 |
| Fruit | 13 | 25.3 |
| Vegetables | 21.5 | 30.7 |
| Brown bread (including wholemeal) | 5.2 | 8 |

Source: Household Food Consumption and Expenditure 1984, Annual Report of the National Food Survey Committee, HMSO.

'Without peace and social justice, without enough food and water, without education and decent housing, and without providing each and all with a useful role in society and adequate income, there can be no health for the people, no real growth and no social development.

Source: Targets for Health for All, World Health Organization 1985.

# PART TWO
# WELFARE

'Welfare' embraces all those essentials that we require to function within a civilised society — not just food, but clothing, housing, and education. In practice, different welfare problems can often be reduced to just one — income/poverty. The reason people don't have proper food, clothing, housing, etc. is often simply that they don't have the money to buy them.

Most people's standards of living in the United Kingdom are definitely rising. But the numbers of poor and low-paid have also risen substantially in the 1980s. In fact, their numbers are so great that predictions that our society will slowly divide into a highly skilled, information-rich overclass, and a permanent, generally impoverished underclass, no longer seem quite as absurd or exaggerated as they once did.

# THE POOR

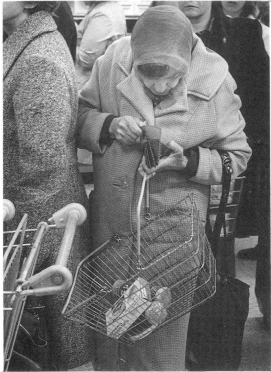

**5,570,000 pensioners (36%)**

**3,750,000 unemployed (24%)**

## 15,420,000
## were living in, or on, the
## margins of poverty (UK, 1985)

i.e. with an income of 140% or less of
Supplementary Benefit (now Income Support)
level. In April 1988, for a single person over 25
that was the equivalent of £46.76 a week or less
(after housing costs).

## 9,380,000
## were living in poverty (UK, 1985)

i.e. were living on or below Supplementary

Benefit level, equivalent (in April 1988 terms) for
a single person over 25 to £33.40 a week or less.

### What is poverty?
Most people agree that poverty should be
defined in relative rather than absolute terms.
Poverty is now seen as a matter of lacking
enough not simply to eat and exist, but to live and
participate in the life of the community.

It's hard though to analyse poverty further in
terms of lifestyle, and lack of clothes, heating,
transport, credit, etc. The most practical course is
to define it simply as some level of income. Two
levels are normally used by social scientists. The
lower is the level of Income Support, which
replaced Supplementary Benefit in April 1988,
and which many accept as the poverty level. The

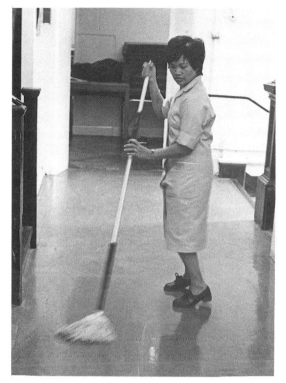

**2,900,000 low paid (19%)**

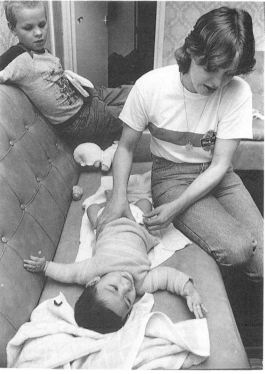

**3,200,000 'others' (31%) (including sick, disabled, single parents, etc.)**

higher is 140% or less of Income Support which is usually termed 'living in or near the margins of poverty'. Both levels are problematic in that Income Support varies for different people.

INCOME SUPPORT
(April 1988)

| | Income Support (cash per week after housing) | 140% of Income Support level |
|---|---|---|
| Single person under 25 | £26.05 | £36.47 |
| Single person over 25 | £33.40 | £46.76 |
| Couple | £51.45 | £72.03 |
| One-parent family with child under 11 | £54.00 | £75.60 |
| Two-parent family with two children under 11 | £79.10 | £110.74 |

The government is opposed to using Income Support as a measure because, as it points out, raising the level of Income Support can have the paradoxical effect of raising the number of poor by increasing the number of those eligible for such financial aid. In addition, Mr Moore, Social Security Secretary, aroused a storm of debate in May 1989 when he argued that today's poor enjoy 'affluence beyond the wildest dreams' of the Victorian poor, since many possess 'luxuries' such as TVs, fridges, videos and even cars.

Certainly the numbers of poor should be treated with some scepticism; they can change markedly in quite short periods. But, according to the Bishop of Stepney in London's East End and many others who replied to Mr Moore, while today's poverty may be different from that portrayed by Dickens, it is just as real — 'the poverty of despair, of discouragement of scraping by, Giro to Giro'.

# THE POOR

## Who?

The 15,420,000 people living in or near poverty in 1985 consisted of: 5,570,000 pensioners (36%), 3,750,000 unemployed (24%), 2,900,000 low-paid (19%), and 3,200,000 'others' (27%), including sick and disabled, single parents, students, people temporarily away from work and carers.

These categories can overlap (although that is considered in the figures). Many pensioners are disabled. Single parents can be low-paid or unemployed. Bear in mind too that the above categories refer only to *poor* pensioners and unemployed, not all pensioners and unemployed.

> Among these groups were 6,450,000 people living in families, including 3,540,000 children (2,250,000 on or below SB level).

## Who receives benefits?

13,820,000 people were dependent on means-tested Social Security benefits in 1985 (one in four of the population).

## Life on the dole

A DHSS survey carried out in 1982 found that of couples with children living on SB, 56% ran out of money most weeks, 70% experienced a period of acute anxiety about money problems, 63% lacked a complete standard set of clothing and 56% were in debt. Unemployed couples with children suffered most.

Source: R. Berthoud, 'The reform of supplementary benefit', Policy Studies Institute 1984.

## Take-up of benefits

Not all of those eligible for Social Security benefits claim them. In 1983, for example, only 76% of those eligible claimed Supplementary Benefit, an average loss of £8.40 per week. A potential £570 million was not claimed.

Source: House of Commons Hansard 30.10.86.

> 'The continuation of high unemployment, low pay and mass dependence on social security benefits bears witness to the persistence of widespread poverty.'
>
> Source: Poverty — The Facts, Child Poverty Action Group, 1988.

## Trends

There are no arguments that poverty increased massively between 1979 and the mid-1980s, only about how much. In 1979 there were 11,570,000 living in or on the margins of poverty, compared with 15,420,000 in 1985. The DHSS argued that 50% of the jump can be accounted for by the rise in the real value of Supplementary Benefit. Even so, it's a steep jump, and the Child Poverty Action Group argues that the DHSS proposed an absolute definition of poverty that does not rise in line with living standards.

The numbers of people, especially children, living *on* the Supplementary Benefit/Income Support line have increased sharply since 1979. But the numbers of pensioners and others living *below* that poverty line have decreased.

> The rich have done much better in the eighties than the poor. The top 10% of income earners had an average rise in real income of 18% between 1979 and 1985, compared with only 6% for the bottom 10%.
>
> Source: House of Commons Hansard, 29.7.1988.

SOURCES: Poverty — The Facts, Childhood Poverty Action Group 1988; Low Income Families Statistics 1988; Households below Average Income, 1981-5, DHSS May 1988.

# THE POOR: DEBT

## 22,630
**mortgages repossessed**
## 89,000
**electricity disconnections**
## 61,000
**gas disconnections
(UK, 1987)**

Sources: House of Commons Hansard 27.6.88, 4.2.88, 13.7.88; Property Market Report, Inland Revenue, Autumn 1988.

As credit has boomed (with the amount of money borrowed doubling in the past seven years) so has the number of debts. It is, of course, mainly the poor, especially those with children, who are in difficulties — though the more affluent can also fall into debt. The commonest debts are fuel and housing arrears. 80,000 households were in arrears on mortgage repayments and in danger of being repossessed in the autumn of 1988.

## Who?
Overwhelmingly, it is lone parents and unemployed families with children who find it difficult to meet their needs and fall into debt. One in four Supplementary Benefit/Income Support claimants are in debt at any one time (including half of those with children).

## Council tenants
Almost a third of council tenants in England and Wales, and nearly a half in Greater London, were behind with their rent in 1987.

Source: House of Commons Hansard 1.7.88.

## How much?
12% of all benefit claimants and 22% of couples with children owe more than £500.

## Suicide
Stuart Giles, founder of Support in Debt, estimates that about one person a day actually commits suicide because of debt.

Source: Support in Debt.

## International comparison
Britain comes top of the EEC for debt, with repayments of interest per capita 80% higher than the next country, France. We also own more credit cards — 34% Britons have a card against the EEC average of 18%.

Source: Mintel, May 1989.

## Trends
The 1987 number of repossessed properties (22,630) was nearly nine times the 1979 total of 2,530.

SOURCE: Building Societies Association 1988.
Source: Credit, Debt and Poverty, HMSO March 1989.

# UNEMPLOYED

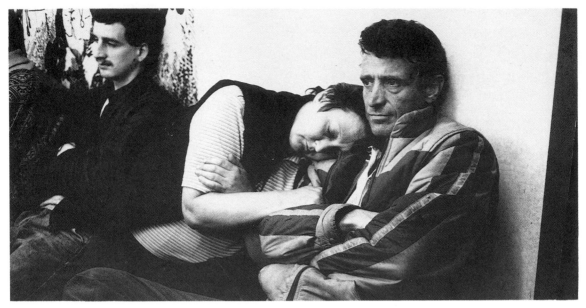

**Supplementary Benefit office, central London**

## 1,988,100
## unemployed (UK, January 1989)

In January 1989, unemployment finally fell through the 2 million barrier, after steadily decreasing for over two years, and the unemployment rate fell to 7%. It was the culmination of steady economic expansion through the mid-eighties, which had seen 2,100,000 new jobs created between March 1983 and March 1988.

But even the seasonally adjusted figure of 2 million is far above what any political party would have been prepared to countenance in the 1970s. And the government has changed the method of counting the unemployed 24 times, excluding many groups such as the Under-18s and Males over-60, raising claims that official figures do not entirely reflect the reality. The

Unemployment Unit regularly produces an alternative count of the unemployed which shows that unemployment increased by 135% between April 1979 and April 1988, compared with official figures of 89%.

Sources: Great Britain, 1989; Child Poverty Action Group; Unemployment Unit; Hansard 25.7.1988.

## Who?

**M/F.** 1,405,700 men, and 582,400 women were unemployed in the UK in January 1989. But many women choose not to register. Many married women stop signing on after a year because they are no longer entitled to Unemployment Benefit or Supplementary Benefit, if, for example, their husband is working. And in 1986, an estimated 340,000 of women classed as economically inactive would have liked work but did not seek it, because they believed no jobs were available.

Source: Labour Force Survey 1986; Social Trends, 1988.

# UNEMPLOYED

**Age.** Unemployment was particularly high among the young and the over-50s: there were 595,700 unemployed 18—24-year-olds (29% of the total unemployed) and 401,300 unemployed 50—59-year-olds (190% of the total).

**Class.** Higher social classes have lower unemployment — 3.5% of professional and managerial workers were unemployed, compared with 22% of general labourers and 9.8% of other manual workers, in mid-1987. But many of the unemployed are well-qualified. While only 4% of the unemployed had a degree in 1986, compared with 45% who had no qualification, some 19% had an A level or equivalent.

Source: Labour Force Survey 1986, Department of Employment; House of Commons Hansard 27.7.88.

**Race.** Pakistani and Bangladeshi men are nearly three times as likely to be unemployed as white workers. For women the figure is four times as high.

Source: Employment Gazette, March 1988.

---

## Long-term unemployed

The unemployment problem may prove increasingly difficult to crack. **821,400 had been unemployed for over a year — 41% of the total in January 1989.** Even worse, 410,700 had been unemployed for over three years, and 133,800 for two to three years.

---

## Effects
All research shows that prolonged unemployment leads to sadness, hopelessness, lack of energy, loss of self-esteem, and increased smoking and drinking. In addition, 16% of unemployed people reported a long-standing illness limiting their activities, compared with 11% of those working (and 36% of those economically inactive).

Source: Social Trends 1989.

## Regions
The variations are very wide, with London and the South doing, and having consistently done, far better than the North and extremities of the country:

| | |
|---|---|
| East Anglia | 4.9% |
| South East | 5.2% |
| South West | 6.8% |
| Wales | 11.5% |
| Scotland | 12.1% |
| North | 12.6% |
| N. Ireland | 18.0% |

There are also great inequalities within regions. In April 1988, for example, the unemployment rate in Tottenham in London was 21%, compared with 3.8% in Sevenoaks in Kent.

## International comparison
Our unemployment rate, which in 1986 was one of the highest in Europe, is now lower than the EEC average, and lower than that of France, Italy, the Netherlands, Belgium and Canada. But we have some way to go to match the record of Japan (2.3%), Sweden (1.7%) and Switzerland (0.7%).

## Trends
We have grown used over the last decade to much higher levels of unemployment. In 1971, there were only 751,000 unemployed claimants, in 1979 there were 1,296,000. The peak came in 1986 with an annual average of 3,289,000.

SOURCE: Employment Gazette, Department of Employment, March 1989.

# LOW-PAID

## 9,050,000
## low-paid workers (GB, April 1988)

i.e. earning £132.27 per week or less, full-time, or £3.50 an hour or less, part-time, **a rate of 44% of the adult workforce**.

Not all the low-paid, by any means, classify as poor. Compare the above rate of £132.27 per week with supplementary benefit at the time of £125.55 for a two-adult, two-child household.

But the low-paid are not far from poverty and they form an enormous percentage of the adult workforce, shattering any notion of Britain being an affluent society.

## What is low pay?

The Low Pay Unit defines it as earnings below two-thirds of average (median) earnings for adult men, which in April 1987 was equal to £132.27 per week or less (for a working week of 37.7 hours) and equivalent to £3.50 an hour or less for part-time workers.

This is higher than the TUC's low pay target of £123.67 (two-thirds of average male manual earnings), but lower than the Council of Europe's £135.35 'decency threshold' (68% of full-time mean earnings).

## Who?

**Part-time workers.**   4,030,000 part-time workers are low-paid. Part-time work and low pay are almost synonymous; four out of five part-time workers were low-paid in 1987.

**M/F.**   Most low-paid workers — about two-thirds — are women. They form the majority of low-paid full-timers (2,660,000 against

2,370,000 men) and the vast majority of part-timers (3,360,000, against 670,000 men). Many are mothers, especially those with young children; 62% of female part-time workers had dependent children, according to the General Household Survey, 1985.

> Over a half (51.9%) of all female full-time employees are low-paid.

## Occupations

Typical low-paying occupations are those within the service sector, such as retail work, catering, cleaning and hotel work.

## Regions

The lowest-paid earn significantly more in London than the rest of the country, though this is offset by the higher cost of living in the capital. The bottom fifth of earners earn around £120 a week in London and £102.50 in the rest of the South East, compared with about £96 per week in most other regions (from £94.20 in Wales and the East Midlands to £97.30 in the North West).

Source: Department of Employment, New Earnings Survey 1987.

## Effects of social security changes

If people leave employment 'voluntarily', they can now only claim unemployment benefit after 6 months rather than 13 weeks. The Low Pay Unit argues that this will leave many low paid workers open to exploitation by unscrupulous employers who know they dare not quit voluntarily.

## A minimum wage?

**There is no minimum wage in the UK** although there is in the USA, France, Netherlands, Spain, and Belgium. The TUC's long-term target for a minimum wage is two-thirds of average earnings for male manual workers, which would currently be in the region of £200.

Source: TUC.

## Trends

The low-paid have increased by 1½ million since 1979, from only 36% of the adult workforce, to 44% today. Their numbers are still growing.

SOURCE: The Poor Decade, Low Pay Unit 1988.

**Mill worker**

# POOR PENSIONERS

**Birmingham pensioner**

## 5,570,000
## pensioners were living in or
## on the margins of poverty
## (GB, 1985)

i.e. had an income of 140% or less of Income Support equivalent for a single pensioner in April 1988 to £57.60 a week or less, in Britain.

Not all pensioners, of course, are poor, but most are — i.e. they live on 140% of Income Support level. In the past, pensioners constituted the vast bulk of the poor. It was only in the eighties that they came to be outnumbered by the armies of unemployed.

Poor pensioners are an ever-growing 'problem' as people live longer and the numbers of elderly swell. Many complain that they deserve better after a lifetime of work. Even those who have made special provision for their old age can find themselves struggling to make ends meet, as the case study below shows.

# POOR PENSIONERS

## Who?

**All pensioners.** Over *half* of all pensioners are poor. In 1985, 9,300,000 people received a pension. The total elderly population is estimated at around 10 million.

Sources: Reform of Social Security, Green Paper 1985; Help the Aged.

**M/F.** Women are far more likely to be poor pensioners. They constitute *two-thirds* of all pensioners, with almost *two* women for every man among the 75-84s, and *three* to one for the over-85s.

Sources: Social Trends 1989; Help the Aged.

## How poor?

Roughly *half* of poor pensioners are living on Income Support level. There are 1,900,000 pensioners on Income Support, and 1,000,000 pensioners who are eligible for, but don't claim, Income Support.

The rest is made up of 2,700,000 on up to 140% of Income Support level.

Source: Social Security Statistics 1987.

## Case study

'I have been working since I left school at 14. I thought I'd be financially secure in my twilight years, but here I am barely managing to break even every week. It hardly seems worth all the planning.'

The *Sunday Times* provided an interesting study of a 69 year old woman pensioner in 1988, quoted above, with a net weekly income of just under £80, derived from both a state and an occupational pension. After paying for rent, rates, tax, utilities, food and clothing, she has only a few pence left at the end of the week for anything other than basic expenses.

Source: Sunday Times, 13.11.1988.

## Where?

**Homes.** Most pensioners live in their own homes. Only 3% live in some form of communal establishment, usually a residential care home, although 19% of the over-85s do.

**Alone.** Over 30% of pensioners live alone — most of whom are women. 43% live in a household with another pensioner.

## Undernourished

About 1-2% of pensioners, around 200,000 people, suffer from serious subnutrition.

Source: W.J. MacLennan, 'Subnutrition in the elderly', British Medical Journal 1986.

## Trends

While the total number of pensioners has grown substantially in recent years, the number of poor pensioners has actually decreased a little. Those living on Supplementary Benefit level, for example, fell by 8% from 3,100,000 in 1979.

Economists argue heatedly about whether pensioners' income has fallen behind or caught up with the rest of the population over the period 1979-85. Either way, the difference is small.

SOURCES: Poverty — The Facts, Childhood Poverty Action Group 1988; Low Income Families Statistics 1988; Households below Average Income, 1981-85, DHSS, May 1988.

# SINGLE-PARENT FAMILIES

## 659,000
## single-parent families were living in or on the margins of poverty (GB, 1986)

i.e. with incomes of 140% or less of Supplementary Benefit/Income Support

As divorces and births outside marriage have increased through the 1970s and 1980s, so has the number of single-parent families left in their wake. **There were 1,010,000 single-parent families in Britain in 1986.** Most are headed by women and most are poor. The great and sometimes insuperable difficulty for single parents is finding work that fits in with childcare — especially if they have babies or toddlers and their local authority doesn't provide daycare facilities.

## Who?

**M/F.**  90% (910,000 families) are headed by women, 10% (100,000) by men.

**Single mothers.**  Contrary to what might be thought, unmarried mothers are a minority of single mothers:

| | |
|---|---|
| 410,000 divorced women | (45%) |
| 190,000 separated women | (21%) |
| 230,000 unmarried women | (25%) |
| 90,000 widows | (10%) |
| (Figures are rounded up.) | |

**Children.**  Over 1,600,000 children are brought up in single-parent families.

## How poor?
The weekly income of all single-parent families, poor and otherwise, in 1986, was on average less than half of that of two-parent families, standing at £120.25 compared with £299.77. Half of lone mothers (51%) cut down on food to save money, according to one study.

Source: H. Graham, Caring for the Family, Health Education Council 1986.

## Where?

**Homes.**  56.2% of all single-parent families lived in properties rented from local authorities in 1986. 28.6% lived in and owned their own homes.

**Regions.**  Single-parent families are most prevalent in London, where they make up 17-19% of all families with children, and 32% in Lambeth. For most of England, Wales and Scotland, the ratio is 11-13%, except for East Sussex, West Midlands, Nottinghamshire, and a few Northern and Scottish counties where the rate is 14-16%.

## Trends
The number of single-parent families has increased almost relentlessly in line with divorces, from 474,000 in 1961, to 570,000 in 1971, to 750,000 in 1976, and 1,010,000 in 1986.

SOURCES: Population Trends 55, HMSO; National Council for One-Parent Families; Households below Average Income, 1981-5, DHSS May 1988; Child Poverty Action Group.

# SINGLE-PARENT FAMILIES

**Homeless 17-year-old with her one-year-old baby, south London**

# CHILDREN IN POVERTY

## 3,540,000 children were living in or on the margins of poverty (GB, 1985)

i.e. on 140% or less of Supplementary Benefit/Income Support level in Britain in 1985.

Vast numbers of children are trapped in poverty. The overall numbers will have dropped somewhat since 1985 due to falling unemployment, but the number of poor children in single-parent families, who constitute a large percentage of the total, has continued to rise. The figure of 3,540,000 constitutes 29% of the total number of children in Britain.

### How poor?

Of the 3.5 million children in or on the margins of poverty in 1985, 2,250,000 (18% of all children) were living on or below the poverty line of Supplementary Benefit level, and 360,000 (3% of all children) were actually living below it.

Source: House of Commons Hansard 15.7.88.

### Who?

Some children were far more at risk of poverty than others. **65% of children in single-parent families — 960,000 — were living on or below the Supplementary Benefit level** compared to only 12% (1,290,000) of children in two-parent families.

### Effects

According to one study, in four out of 10 poor families, children have to go without meals, are ill protected against the cold, and normally wear second-hand clothes (particularly distressing to teenagers), for lack of money to pay for food, heating and new clothes.

Sources: L. Burghes, 'Children in Poverty', Concern, National Children's Bureau 1984.

SOURCES: Low Income Families Statistics, 1985, DHSS, May 1988; Child Poverty Action Group.

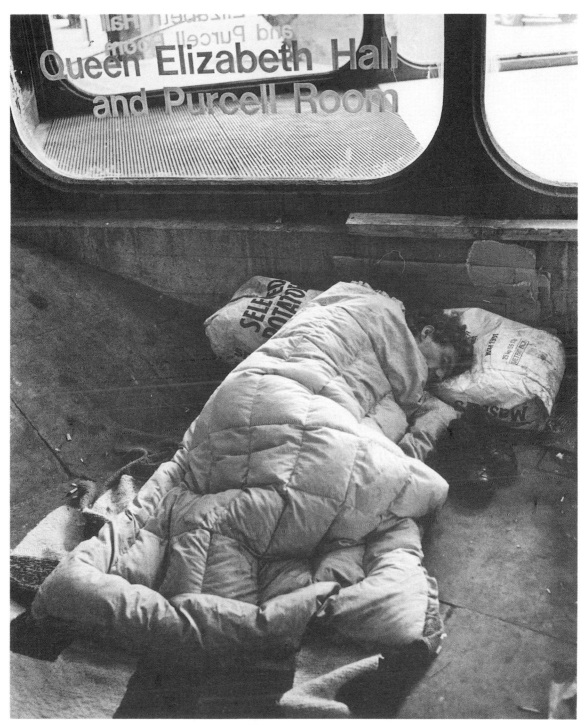

**Sleeping rough in the South Bank Arts Complex, London**

# HOMELESS

## 430,000
## homeless people (GB, 1987)

The above total, it has to be stressed, covers all people becoming homeless over the year. At any one time, the total may have been more in the region of 100,000. It's a total derived from estimates for both homeless *households* accepted by local authorities, and *single* homeless. (Single people and childless couples are very rarely accepted by authorities.)

Homelessness in all forms has been steadily increasing over the last two decades, swollen by the general economic conditions and, in the 1980s, by a decreasing stock of public housing as more and more council dwellings are sold off.

The situation is now acute. Local authorities have a statutory duty to house the homeless in priority need. But inner city councils, according to the Audit Commission, have become so overstretched by demands from the homeless that they will soon be unable to cope.

More recently, large numbers of young people are becoming homeless and literally roofless as a result of the changes to Social Security benefits in April 1988. If Shelter's more recent estimate of 150,000 single homeless in 1988 is correct, the homeless total for 1989 may well be over 500,000.

Source: Audit Commission 1988.

# SINGLE HOMELESS

## 64,500
## single homeless people in London (end of 1987)

There is no official collection of statistics on the single homeless — the above total is only for London. The numbers of homeless, especially the young, have grown dramatically since the Social Security changes of 1988. Under these changes, Income Support is no longer paid to 16- and 17-year-olds except in very special cases. Thus many youngsters have no source of income if they can't find a Youth Training Scheme place or a job. And they can fall into a vicious circle if they become homeless, because then it's even harder for them to get and hold down a YTS place. Hence what seems like an epidemic of roofless young people begging on the streets of London.

The legislation does not seem to consider that domestic circumstances often force young people out on the streets with nowhere to go.

**A central London hostel**

---

### There were 150,000 single homeless people in Britain in early 1989.

Shelter's estimate was extrapolated from a 17% sample of local authorities counting the numbers of single people who had applied to them for help and been turned down.

Source: Shelter, March 1989; Children in Danger, National Children's Home Factfile 1989.

---

### Where?
In London, at the end of 1987, 2,000 were sleeping rough; 30,000 were squatting; 15,000 were living in short-life condemned property; 10,000 were living in night shelters or direct access hospitals; and 7,500 were in Bed and Breakfast hotels.

### Effects of social security changes
The benefit changes of April 1988 have contributed to homelessness in ways that do not only affect 16-17-year-olds. 18-25-year-olds had their benefit rates cut to a very low £26.05. And Income Support is now paid up to two weeks in arrears, where Supplementary Benefit was paid in advance. One case illustrates the consequences. A woman released from prison was refused a crisis loan. When her probation officer protested, he was told: 'We're turning people away if they have slept rough before — they can sleep rough again.'

Source: True Horror Stories: Central London Social Security Advisers' Forum, November 1988.

SOURCES: New Year 1988, Another Disastrous Year for London's Homeless, London Housing Unit, 31 December 1987; Shelter 1989.

# HOMELESS HOUSEHOLDS

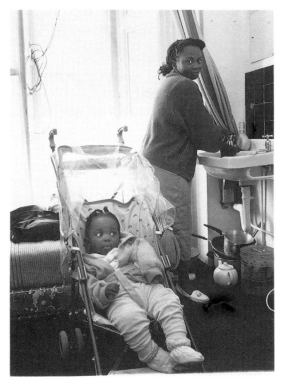

**Mother and child placed in private Bed and Breakfast, Earls Court, London**

# 128,345
## homeless households, a total of 370,000 people (GB, 1987)

The first figure here is the official total for the households homeless, or threatened with homelessness, for whom Britain's local authorities accepted responsibility in 1987. Authorities do not count all the individual members. Shelter has estimated their number at 370,000 on the basis of a government survey.

Source: survey, Angela Evans and Sue Duncan, Responding to Homelessness, Local Authority Policy and Practice, Department of the Environment 1988.

## Who?
91% of homeless households accepted by authorities in England and Wales in 1987 were 'in priority need'. 64% were adults with 'one or more dependent children'. Others included pregnant women, and people vulnerable because of old age, physical handicap, or mental illness, but not the vast mass of single homeless.

All research agrees that homeless households are all extremely poor. London Housing News quotes Department of Environment figures showing that only 21% are employed and 70% are reliant on welfare benefits.

Source: London Housing News, January 1989.

## Why?
Some of the most common reasons for households becoming homeless in Great Britain in 1986 were:

- parents, relatives or friends no longer willing to accommodate (40% of cases);
- breakdown of relationship with partner (20%);
- court orders for mortgage default or rent arrears (14%)

Shelter stresses that in most cases these are reasons that cannot be foreseen.

## Council housing stock
The national supply of council lettings has fallen from 274,000 in 1980, to 243,000 in 1986. The Audit Commission has calculated that the cost of building a council home is only £7,400 a year, while that of keeping a family in Bed and Breakfast is £11,315 a year.
'In 1987 the number of homeless households accepted by local authorities in London was greater than the number of available lettings for the first time.'

Sources: Audit Commission 1988; Shelter's Christmas Report on Homelessness 1988.

# HOMELESS HOUSEHOLDS

## Temporary housing

There were about 25,000 accepted homeless households in temporary accommodation in England and Wales: 10,000 in Bed and Breakfast hotels; 5,000 in hostels (including women's refuges); and 10,000 in short-life tenancies.

## Bed and Breakfast

Such accommodation, which is often substandard, can create great stresses within families, as well as causing poor health and isolation from the rest of the community. Many families are placed away from their own borough, and find it hard fully to use the medical, social and educational services. There are about 12,000 children in London Bed and Breakfast accommodation, who find it hard to enrol at, or succeed in, local schools.

In 1988, London's local authorities spent £100 million on B & B, compared with £12 million in 1985.

Sources: New Year 1988, Another Disastrous Year for London's Homeless, London Housing Unit, 31 December 1987; Shelter 1989.

## Home ownership

While homelessness has increased, so has home ownership. Owner-occupied homes doubled between 1961 and 1987 from 7 million to 14.5 million.

## Trend

Homelessness has been growing alarmingly over the last two decades, from just 7,652 homeless households in 1970, in the whole of the UK, to 56,750 in 1979, to the present total.

SOURCES: Social Trends 1988, 1989.

**North London hotel**

# POOR HOUSING

## 463,000
### dwellings (2.5%) lack basic amenities

i.e. did not have one or more of the following: an indoor WC, bath, sink & wash basin, with hot and cold water supply. (England and Wales, 1986.)

## 900,000
### dwellings (4.8%) were unfit to live in

i.e. 'unsuitable for human habitation' according to nine criteria, such as repair, stability, freedom from damp.

**Liverpool maisonettes**

# POOR HOUSING

## 2,400,000 dwellings (12.9%) were in poor repair

i.e. needed urgent repairs to the external fabric of the property estimated to cost over £1,000.

There are now only 139,000 dwellings without that mainstay of civilisation, the indoor loo. But improvements to the housing stock, which have been immense over the century as a whole, have not been so dramatic in the eighties. There is still a lot of poor housing, occupied, not surprisingly, mainly by the poor — especially the elderly, ethnic minorities, and the unemployed.

It has been estimated that £86.5 billion is needed to repair and improve housing and meet urgent needs.

Source: The Association of Metropolitan Authorities Housing Facts 1988.

> ### All Dwellings
> in England totalled 18,800,000 in 1986. Half were built before 1944, a quarter before 1919. Most — 16,300,000 — were in urban areas.

## Who?

**Income.**   The English House Condition Survey 1986 found that: 'Poor housing was related, above all, to income. Half of all households lacking amenities, one-third of those in unfit housing and 27% of those whose homes were in poor repair had net incomes of less than £3,000. The majority of these households lived in rented accommodation.'

**Age.**   Elderly households (headed by someone over 75) were three times more likely to be without basic amenities than others, and one and a half times more likely to be in unfit dwellings.

**Race.**   A high proportion of households where the head was born in the New Commonwealth live in poor condition dwellings — 9.3% were in unfit housing, as against only 3.8% where the household head was born in the UK.

## Where?

**Regions.**   There are more dwellings in poor condition in the North West (16%), the South East including London (15.7%), Yorkshire and Humberside (12%) and the West Midlands (11.8%) than in other regions, especially Inner London (6.1%) and East Anglia (4.1%). This is often a reflection of the age of housing stocks. Privately owned slum terraces in the North have been targetted as one of the most urgent housing problems.

Source: Independent, 11.6.1988.

**Rural.**   22% of rural housing is in poor condition against 14% in urban areas — partly to be explained by the higher proportion of older homes (40% against 25%).

> ### Half of all local authority flats were affected by litter, graffiti or vandalism, extensively so in 10% of these cases.

## Trends

England's housing stock has improved somewhat since 1981. Then 5% (double the 1986 number of houses) lacked basic amenities and more were unfit — 6.3% against 4.8%, but the extent of poor repair has remained much the same.

SOURCE: English House Condition Survey, 1986, HMSO.

# EDUCATION

While there are, and always have been, many who complain about falling educational standards, students have actually been getting better results (though it is too early to measure the impact of the new GCSE). More places have been made available at nearly all levels of education, including places for mature students (an area where we may well see major expansion in years to come).

But our educational system looks very backward when compared with our industrial competitors. And as a comparison of the results of independent and state sectors shows, there is room for massive improvement.

> **'As a nation, we have extraordinarily low expectations of the majority of our children.'**
> H.M. Inspectors of Schools report,
> 1.3.1989

## EXAM RESULTS
## NO O-LEVELS/CSEs:
## 11% of school leavers
## NO A-LEVELS/HIGHERS:
## 81% of school leavers
## (UK, 1986-87)

It must be stressed that these figures refer to *all* school leavers, including both state and independent school leavers. Almost 19% of school leavers in 1986-87 had one or more A-levels (and almost 15% had two or more).

About 53% had at least 1 GCE O-level (grades A-C) or equivalent, with about 10% gaining five or more, and almost 27% gaining between one and four.

### Who?

**M/F.** More boys (12.7%) left without any O-levels or other graded results than girls (9.1%). Fewer boys (34.2%) than girls (41%) got one or more O-levels (grades A — C) or equivalent. But the proportions of boys (18.6%) and girls (18.9%) getting A-levels were roughly the same.

### Regions

There are some marked differences between performances throughout the nation. In 1985-86, for example, only 10.8% of boys in England left without any O-levels or graded results, compared with 18.4% in Wales, 26.2% in Scotland, and 27.4% in Northern Ireland.

Source: Regional Trends 1988.

### Trends

Performance has improved a little at all levels in education over the last 10 years. 15% of boys got two or more A-levels (or equivalent) in 1986-87, for example, compared with only 14.3% in 1975-76. 9.5% of boys got five or more O-levels or equivalent compared with 7.2% in 1975-6.

The most dramatic improvement has been the reduction in those getting no grades of any description from around 20% in 1975-76 to under 11% in 1986-87.

SOURCE: Social Trends 1989.

## PROVISION
## 25%
## of 18-24-year olds were in further or higher education (UK, 1986-87)

'Further education' covers students at polytechnics, colleges and other institutions studying for A-levels and diplomas of a similar level. 'Higher education' covers students at universities and polytechnics studying for anything above A-level.

### Where?
4% of 18-24-year-olds were at university, 6% in polytechnics and colleges, 15% in further education.

### International comparison
Our staying-on rate is far below that of most other western countries. In 1981, for example, when we had 48% of our 16-18-year-olds staying on in full-time education, W. Germany had 61%, Japan 87%, the Netherlands 90%, and the USA 94%.

Source: Statistical Bulletin, September 1985, Department of Education.

### Trends
The numbers of full-time students in higher education have risen by 15% since 1980-81 to reach 613,000 in 1986-87. The main increases have been in polytechnics and colleges; university intake has barely changed. The numbers of part-time students have risen much more dramatically, more than doubling from 165,000 in 1970-71 to 359,000 in 1986-87 — the increase coming almost entirely from those aged over 25. 10% of all graduates now come from the Open University each year.

## 45%
## of 16-year-olds stayed on in full-time education (UK, 1987)

The number of 16- and 17-year-olds who stay on in full-time education compares very poorly with the UK's industrial competitors. Full-time education embraces students both in schools and in further and higher education institutions. It should be distinguished from part-time education — there are also many students on part-time courses in further and higher education.

### Other 16-year-olds
While 45% stayed on in 1987 (31% at school and about 15% in various forms of further education), 17% were employed, 11% were unemployed, and 27% were on the Youth Training Scheme (YTS).

### Regions
There are some regional variations — 51% of 16-year-olds stayed on in full-time education in the South East in 1985-86, compared with only 39.8% in the North.

Source: Regional Trends 1988.

### Trends
The proportion of 16-year-olds staying on has risen from 40% in 1976 to 45% in 1987.

SOURCE: Social Trends 1989.

# EDUCATION

## 19%
## of all under-5s had daycare places (UK, 1986)

Our provision of school and daycare places for under-5s is not very generous, especially when considering that nearly half of children attending school were part- rather than full-time, and around two-thirds of daycare places were in playgroups. The UK needs many more places if mothers are to be free to re-enter the workforce earlier.

### Regions
There were wide variations in regional provision of school places for under-5s in 1986 from Wales, the highest, where 69.1% of 3- and 4-year-olds were in maintained schools, down to the South East and South West, where only 33.1% and 29.4% were provided for.

Source: Regional Trends 1988.

### Trends
The proportion of children, aged 3 to 4, attending school in the UK has risen from 15% in 1966 to 48% in 1987. Daycare places for under-5s, including playgroups, day nurseries and registered childminders, have risen from 128,000 places in 1966, to 722,000 in 1987.

SOURCE: Social Trends 1989.

## CLASS SIZE
## 21 pupils:
## average class size in secondary schools (England, 1987)
## 26 pupils:
## average class size in primary schools

The above figures are only average class sizes, but the variations are not great. Only 5% of classes in secondary schools had 31 or more pupils, 46% had 20 pupils or less, 45% had 21-30. 18% of primary school classes had 31 pupils or more. 76% had less than 30. (A few classes at all levels had two or more teachers).

### Trends
Class sizes have generally been getting smaller — the averages falling from 22 for secondary schools in 1977 to 21 in 1987, and from 27 for primary schools in 1977 to 26 in 1987.

SOURCE: Social Trends 1989.

## STATE vs INDEPENDENT SCHOOLS

Independent schools, which now account for 7% of the total educational system of the UK, outperform maintained schools by staggering margins at both A- and O-level. On the other hand, the more specialist schools and sectors of the maintained system come very much closer to independent schools.

### Performance

**A-Levels.** 65% of school leavers at independent schools had one or more A-levels, compared to 14% at state schools. 46% had three or more A-levels, against 8% in the state sector.

INDEPENDENT SCHOOLS: 65% of school leavers have one or more A-levels

STATE SCHOOLS: 14% of school leavers have one or more A-levels

**O-Levels.** The independent sector outperformed the state sector — 73.8% of their leavers had five or more O-levels, against only 23% in maintained schools.

## State 'specialists'

Much closer to independent schools were *sixth form colleges*, where 54% of leavers had one or more A-levels, and 68% had five or more O-levels, and *grammar schools*, where the corresponding figures were 59.3% and 79.4% (the last of which was actually *better* than independent schools).

## Oxbridge entrance

In 1988, state schools gained only 43% and 46% of acceptances to Cambridge and Oxford respectively, compared with independent schools' 45% and 46%. (Overseas, mature and other students accounted for the rest.)

Sources: Cambridge University Reporter, no. 13; Oxford Colleges Admission Office.

## Class size

One factor in the success of independent schools is much smaller classes. Their average teacher-pupil ratio was 1:11.

SOURCES: Department of Education and Science; Independent Schools Information Service.

## Trends

The numbers being educated in independent sector schools are increasing, up from 5.6% of all pupils in 1979 to 7% in 1989.

# ADULT LITERACY

# ADULT LITERACY

## 13% of all adults have basic skills difficulties
## 1% are illiterate

The above figures must be carefully qualified. They are from an extensive survey of 23-year-olds in 1981 by the National Child Development Study, which tracks all those born in a certain week in 1958. It suggests that a considerable number of adults have self-perceived *difficulties* with reading, writing and basic numeracy, but that does not mean they are 'illiterate'. Only about 1% of adults interviewed had generalised literacy problems — 'I cannot read or write at all.'

### Difficulties

**Literacy.** 10% of adults interviewed had problems with reading, writing or spelling since leaving school. Contrary to stereotypes, more of those interviewed (9.3%) had difficulties with writing and spelling than with reading (3.8%).

**Numeracy.** 5% of interviewees had difficulties with numeracy, but only 1% had problems with the basic operations of adding, subtracting, multiplying and dividing.

### Effects
Basic skills difficulties particularly prevented people from looking and applying for jobs. Many had problems with letters and forms.

### Who?

**M/F** More men (12%) reported literacy difficulties than women (7%), though equal numbers of both had numeracy difficulties.

SOURCE: Literacy, Numeracy and Adults, a report by the Adult Literacy Basic Skills Unit 1987.

---

### Very poor
We are very poor at simple maths, spelling and reading railway timetables, according to a MORI poll conducted in September 1988, which put a few simple questions to a cross-section of the population. 42% asked to calculated the cost of a burger, chips, pie and coffee from a menu got it wrong; 46% read a railway timetable wrongly in answer to a question; and 59% mis-spelled 'embarrass' and 'satellite'.

Source: Sunday Times, 16.10.1988.

# PART THREE
# RELATIONSHIPS

Only the most basic relationships are covered here — family and marriage. In principle, we could also deal with friendships and other kinds of relationship, but statistics are hard to come by on such matters. The categories covered raise enough difficulties anyway — should divorces and non-marital births, for example, be considered as problems at all?

The numbers of both divorces and illegitimate births have been accelerating in the last two decades, as the bonds of marriage and family have loosened.

# DIVORCE

## 165,000 divorces (UK, 1987)

The divorce rate has risen fairly steadily for the last 30 years, so that if present trends continue roughly **one in three marriages will end in divorce**. (There were 398,000 marriages in 1987.) Partly this is because divorce has been made increasingly easy by legal changes, partly it is because our society no longer holds the bonds of family as quite so sacred as it once did.

Divorces may, from the point of view of the partners, be very desirable. But they can be harmful for the children involved, as the study below indicates. And as the divorce rate has risen, so have the numbers of single-parent families, most of whom are living in or near the margins of poverty.

## Who?

**M/F.**   73% of divorces were granted to wives in 1987 — the highest proportion ever recorded. Over half of these were on grounds of unreasonable behaviour. The most common reason men were granted divorces was their wives' adultery (45% of cases).

## When?

Since 1961, most divorces have occurred between the fifth and ninth years of marriage. In 1987, 29% of divorces occurred then, with 17.5% between the tenth and fourteenth years — and 4% after *30* years. A *Today* survey of 1,483 adults offered support for these figures, showing that the average time for affairs to begin was the sixth year of marriage (fifth year for men, eighth year for women).

Source: survey, Today, 1.2.89.

## Effects on children

149,000 children under 16 were affected by divorces in 1987 in England and Wales. About 50,000 — 32% — were under the age of 5.

A third of divorced children lose contact with one parent as an immediate result of separation, according to a study by Ann Mitchell published in Family Law in December 1988. Nearly half think the separation is only temporary. Most would prefer to continue living with both their natural parents whatever the domestic situation.

About 44% of divorcees had no children.

Source: OPCS; article, 'One child in two', The Times, 7.12.88.

## Attitudes to divorce

**Only 5% of British people think it is too difficult to get a divorce**; 56% think it is too easy; and 31% think the present system is about right, according to a recent survey, based on a sample of 1,011 adults.

Source: NOP poll, Mail On Sunday, 5.3.89.

## International comparison

Great Britain has the highest divorce rate in the EEC, with 12.6 marriage breakdowns per 1,000 existing marriages, whereas Roman Catholic Italy has just 1.1. But the other countries, especially France, are catching up. Over the 10 years to 1989, the number of divorces rose by 38.7% in the seven largest EEC countries — must faster than the UK.

## Trends

Divorce rates more than doubled in both the 1960s and 1970s, from 2.1 per 1,000 existing marriages in 1961, to 5.8 in 1971, to 11.5 in 1981. In the 1980s, the rise has been much less steep — to a rate of 12.6 in 1987.

SOURCE: OPCS; Statistical Office of the EEC.

# ADOPTION

## 8,904
## adoptions (GB, 1986)

The number of babies put up for adoption has declined dramatically over the last 20 years, partly because it is so much easier to have an abortion, partly because single mothers are keeping their babies.

The focus of adoption agencies has shifted towards placing children with 'special needs' such as mentally and/or physically handicapped children, and children from ethnic backgrounds who are much more difficult for the social services to place.

The adoption figures are heavily distorted by step-parent adoptions (usually where the mother and a new husband adopt the mother's children from a former relationship). These accounted for over 50% of adoptions between 1980 and 1984.

## Who?

**Age of adoption.** Children of all ages are adopted, not just babies. In 1986 over a quarter were over the age of 10. Only 43% (excluding those adopted by step-parents) were under 1-year-old in 1984 in England and Wales.

**Non-marital births.** 56% of all children adopted in 1986 were born outside marriage.

## Trends
Adoptions in England and Wales have fallen steeply from 24,831 in 1968 to 7,892 in 1986, and even more dramatically if step-parent adoptions are excluded, from 16,314 in 1968 to 4,189 in 1984.

SOURCES: OPCS; General Register Office (Scotland); British Agencies for Adoption and Fostering.

# CHILDREN IN CARE

## 82,000
## children in care (GB, 1987)

Children come into the care of local authorities both voluntarily and committed by the courts. They come for a variety of reasons, including illness and desertion or death of parents, prolonged physical or sexual abuse, and severe emotional deprivation.

Their numbers have been steadily falling, and they are increasingly living in the community rather than in children's homes. 52% of children were boarded out with foster parents in England in March 1987, compared with only a third in 1977. Those in community homes have fallen from about a third in 1974 in England and Wales, to about a fifth in 1987. But there is a shortage of carers, especially for 'emergency fostering' on a short-term basis, and for teenagers.

Many children leaving care have been in a desperate situation, according to the Association of Metropolitan Authorities, since the Social Security changes of April 1988. Income Support to 16- and 17-year-olds living in their own tenancies, as for most young people in care, was reduced from £31 to just £19.50 a week. The AMA fears a tragedy and has appealed to Social Security Secretary, John Moore.

### Entering care
58% of children in care in England in March 1986 had been committed by the courts.

### Leaving care
Around 31,600 children left care in England in 1986. In 48% of cases, it was because they had become self-supporting, or the care had been taken over by a parent, guardian, relative or friend. In almost a quarter of cases, it was because they had attained the age of 18 or 19.

### Age
68.4% of children in care in England in March 1987 were 10 or over. 28,300 (42.9%) were aged 10-15. Only 1,600 (2.4%) were under the age of 1.

### Removed
In England in the year ending 31 March 1987, 8,055 children were 'removed to a place of safety,' which is a temporary measure for up to 28 days and does not classify as being in care.

### Regions
Scotland had a higher rate of children in care with 10.4 children per 1,000 population in 1987 (12,517 altogether), compared with a rate of 5.96 in England.)

### Trend
The numbers of children in care have fallen steadily by over 25% since 1979 in England and Wales, from 100,100, to 72,800 in 1985. But the numbers of children removed to a place of safety have increased disturbingly since 1985, and in 1987 at 8,055 were 12% up on the 1986 total of 7,191.

SOURCES: DHSS November 1988; Scottish Education Department 1988; Welsh Office 1988; Children in Danger, National Children's Home Factfile 1989; Voluntary Voice March 1989.

# NON-MARITAL BIRTHS

## 178,000
## non-marital births (UK, 1987)

'Illegitimate' is now an illegal term — as a result of the Family Law Reform Act of 1987, it cannot be used in any laws relating to children born outside marriage. That act defined the correct term as 'non-marital', and gave non-marital children exactly the same rights to inherit as the children of married parents. Previously, they could only inherit from their parents, not other relatives, unless they were specifically mentioned in their wills.

Non-marital births have risen very sharply from 8% of all births in 1971, to 23% in 1986. An increasing number are being registered in joint names — 68% in England and Wales in 1987, against 38% in 1961 — and Social Trends points out that over half of non-marital children will be brought up in a 'stable', two-parent family. Certainly, the social stigma which once attached to both single-parent families and non-marital births has largely been removed.

## Who?

**Race.** The rate of non-marital births is highest among Carribean-born women (48.3% in 1986), and low among Indians (1.7%) and Pakistanis and Bangladeshis (0.6%).

**Regions.** In 1986, Merseyside had the highest rate in the UK with 30.8% of all non-marital births, compared with the UK average of 21%. Cumbria and Greater Manchester were next with 29.9% and 28.6% respectively. London had 24.7%, whereas the Southern region of Northern Ireland had only 8.7%, the lowest for the UK.

## No nationality rights
A child born out of wedlock in Britain after 31 December 1982 cannot claim British citizenship unless the *mother*, and only the mother, is already a British citizen or settled in Britain. It is not enough to have been born here or to have a father who is a British citizen. This is a part of the British Nationality Act of 1981 which the Family Law Reform Act of 1987 did not reform, despite considerable protest.

## Trends

Non-marital births have been rising very rapidly in the eighties, from 12.5% in 1981 to 21% in 1986, and that has been reflected right across the regions. Merseyside's 30.8% in 1986, for example, was up from 18.2% in 1981, and even the Southern region of Northern Ireland's 8.7% had almost doubled from 4.6% in 1981.

SOURCES: Social Trends 1988, 1989; Regional Trends 1988.

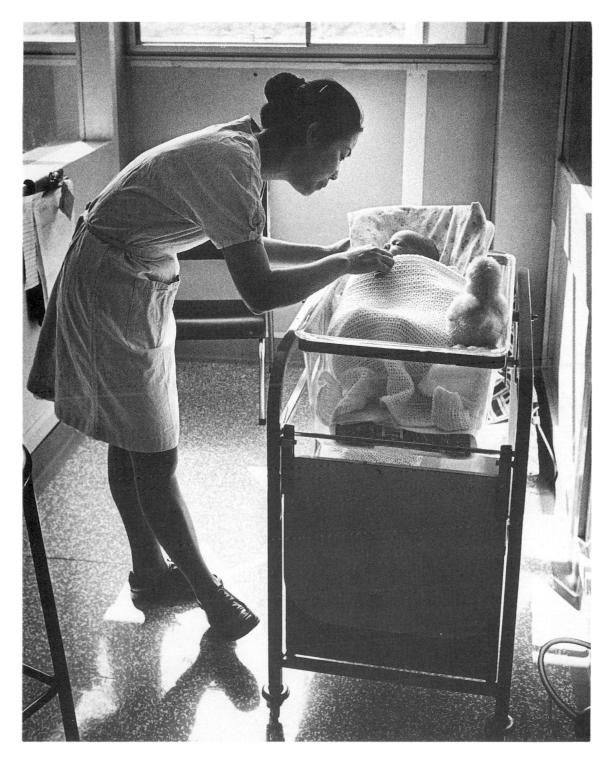

# PART FOUR
# FREEDOM

If welfare is about what we need to live, freedom is about how we are allowed to live. It covers the freedoms and restrictions that a society extends to groups (discrimination) and to all its members, (civil liberties), to engage in the activities of life — such as work, love, political participation, and freedom of speech and information.

The United Kingdom used to be proud of the freedom allowed to its citizens, but in the 1980s has too often found itself hauled up in front of European courts for that pride to be sustained. And civil liberties have arguably been diminished significantly in recent years.

# SEXUAL DISCRIMINATION

Over the last two decades, the women's movement has shown how women experience discrimination in most areas of life in a myriad of forms — from the pay and opportunities offered them at work, to the time and encouragement given them by teachers in education, to the language and images used to depict them by our culture. Much of that discrimination is difficult, if not impossible to measure.

What can be measured are the *results* of discrimination, especially at work. Women's pay and power are still far less than men's. And that cannot be put down to working less, or pushing themselves forward less energetically. Surveys show that women place increasing importance on work, but are often denied equal wages, and held back from promotion.

Women also face massive discrimination when it comes to combining motherhood and career. They may get little or no help from the state with childcare — which is becoming the new 'feminist frontier' — and as yet few companies in the private sector offer 'career break' schemes, supporting women through breaks for motherhood, and enabling them to return to work later.

Things are changing. Women are gaining more power, if not much more pay. And some predict radical changes in the 1990s, when, with a sharp decline in the number of young people entering the workforce, women's contribution should be more highly valued. But the changes are still slow.

## PAY

### The average weekly pay for women in Britain in 1987 was £147.20, 66.2% of the average for men (£222.10)

Based on average gross weekly earnings *including overtime*, for full-time employees, 18 and over.

Women still earn much less than men, although the figures are not so bad when overtime is considered — 18.6% of male employees regularly work paid overtime, compared with only 6.3% of female employees.

Source: Labour Market Quarterly Report, Manpower Services Commission, September 1987.

### The average hourly pay for women in Britain in 1987 was £3.84, 73.6% of the average for men (£5.21)

Based on average gross weekly earnings, *excluding overtime*, for full-time employees, 18 and over.

Source: New Earnings Surveys; Women and Men in Britain, A Statistical Profile, Equal Opportunities Commission, 1987.

### Trends

While women's pay has improved substantially since 1971 when it was only 63.7% of men's, there has been no real improvement since 1979, when it was 73%. It may even be declining.

# SEXUAL DISCRIMINATION

**The food production line at a top London Hospital**

## TOP PAY

### 5.3% of women, and 21.6% of men, earn over £250 a week (after tax, 1987)

0.6% of women, and 5.2% of men, earn over £400 a week (after tax, 1987). A recent survey confirms that women are poorly paid even when they attain professional or managerial status. Although 48% of the respondents were professional women and a third held management positions, only one in five earned more than £15,000 and almost half earned less than £10,000.

Sources: New Earnings Surveys; Employment Gazette, November 1987; survey, Elle magazine, November 1988.

### Remedial action

'Our equal pay laws must be radically strengthened and rigorously enforced if they are to make any impact on the wages discrimination faced by two many women today.' (NCCL)

## Women make up 70% of the poor.

Joni Seager and Ann Olson point out that poverty is being feminized — women-headed households and women pensioners make up, on average, about 70 per cent of the poor in most countries in the world. In Britain they make up:

- 6,020,000 low-paid workers (66% of the total);
- 3,700,000 poor pensioners (66% of the total);
- 623,000 poor single parents (90% of the total).

And that doesn't take into account other categories like poor, unemployed women.

Source: Joni Seager & Ann Olson, Women in the World, London, 1986.

# CEXUAL DISC RIMINATION

## Economic participation

In comparing pay, we also have to consider the extent to which women participate in the economy. The statistics show that women are becoming an ever larger part — nearly a half — of the labour force, and working almost as long hours as men. **Women make up 42.6% of the labour force over the age of 16 (Great Britain, 1988).**

## Hours worked

Women work an average 38.1 hours, and men an average 39.1 hours, a week in manual occupations. Women work an average 36.1 hours, and men an average 37.1 hours, a week in non-manual occupations.

Source: New Earnings Survey, Part F 1986.

---

### Attitude to work

More and more women *want* to work. In an Elle survey:
- only 8% of women said they would like to stop work altogether;
- 63% said they would work even if they did not need the money.

Source: Elle, November 1988.

### Ambition

More and more women want to *succeed.* A survey of 21,000 single women showed that:
- 66% would love to be a high-powered, high-profile woman;
- only 15% said the thought terrified them;
- 18% were attracted by the idea but thought men were put off by high-flying women.

Source: Cosmopolitan, October 1988.

---

## OCCUPATION

## 81% of women are employed in service industries

In the UK, women are largely confined to certain job ghettos, such as:
- secretarial work
- cleaning
- nursing
- social work
- teaching.

In short, they are confined to services which they provide for free at home. They comprise 78% of NHS and 86% of local authority health and personal social services employees. Many, such as nurses and teachers, are widely acknowledged to be appallingly paid for demanding work. Even in areas of training, women are trapped in job ghettoes; 82% of clerical, catering or retail jobs on YTS schemes were done by women.

## Trends

The situation is changing. More and more women are choosing the professions. They account for 47% of medical graduates, and 40% of qualifying solicitors, and, over the last 10 years, the proportion of women members of the Chartered Insurance Institute has risen from 4% to 14%.

Some are predicting that women will fare much better in the 1990s as the numbers of young people entering the workforce decline.

Sources: Social Trends 1988; Alan Walker and Carol Walker, The Growing Divide, Child Poverty Action Group 1987.

# SEXUAL DISCRIMINATION

> An Elle survey found that most women continue to suffer from discrimination, both overt and insidious. 42% claimed they had suffered some form of discrimination, and 60% found that as women they were expected to do things at work that men were not.
>
> Source: Elle, November 1988

## Qualifications

Girls certainly have the qualifications for equal pay and success — they are fast catching up on boys in education if not actually outstripping them.

In 1986, 72% of girls, and 68.7% of boys, passed one or more O-levels (or the equivalent). 18.9% of girls, and 18.6% of boys, passed one or more A-levels (or the equivalent). 62% of all school leavers continuing into further education were girls. 42% of all students following degree courses were women.

## Subject ghettos

There are still some subjects where girls predominate (especially Cookery and to a much lesser extent the Arts) and others where boys predominate (such as the Sciences, Physics, Maths and Technology, although more and more girls are gaining passes in these areas).

Girls had 96% of the passes in Cookery O-level, and 6% of the passes in Technical Drawing O-level, in 1985.

**Chemistry class in grammar school in Grantham, formerly attended by Margaret Thatcher**

# SEXUAL DISCRIMINATION

## POWER

Women are pitifully represented both at the upper levels of organisational hierarchies and in specific seats of power and authority — political, legal, trade union, police, and so on.

## BUSINESS EXECUTIVES

**In the top 100 firms in the UK, *none* of the chief executives are women**, and out of 1,000 directors only eight are women.

In the 1,500 leading companies, only 3% of directors are women.

Source: Directory of Directors; survey, Valerie Hammond, Women in Management in Great Britain, 1988.

## POLITICS

**Out of 650 MPs, only 42 (6.5%) are women.**

The government may be led by a woman prime minister, but out of 22 cabinet ministers, none are women, and out of 85 junior ministers, only four are women (Angela Rumbold — Education; Lynda Chalker — Overseas Development; Virginia Bottomley — Environment; and Gillian Shepherd — Social Services).

The 300 Group, which seeks equal representation for women in Parliament, argues that women's poor representation is no longer due to their failure to put themselves forward as candidates, but rather to the failure of local party committees to select them. The 300 Group also argues that the myth that a woman is unelectable or less electable is strictly a myth.

Source: House of Commons, April 1989.

### International comparison

Britain compares very poorly with Scandinavian countries, where women make up between 24% (Norway) and 32% (Sweden and Finland) of MPs, and not so well with Germany (15%) and Italy (13% of MPs).

Most European governments now have women cabinet ministers, but with portfolios such as Family, Social Welfare and Women's Rights. None is a Minister of Finance, Trade, Economics or Defence.

Source: Women and Men in Great Britain 1987, HMSO.

## JUDICIARY

**Of 79 high court judges, only three are women.** Of 390 circuit judges, only 16 are women. Of 558 recorders, only 23 are women. Of 66 stipendiary magistrates, eight are women.

Source: Lord Chancellor's Department 1987

### Trends

Poor as this is, in 1960 there was only one woman in the entire judiciary — and she was a stipendiary magistrate.

## POLICE

**Only four out of 367 Scotland Yard detectives in October 1988 were women.** 'There is plenty of evidence' of discrimination within Scotland Yard restricting job opportunities for women officers, who make up about 10% of the entire police force. Senior male officers illegally impose quotas on women joining specialist crime squads, limiting them to one or two.

Source: internal Metropolitan Police report leaked to Sunday Times, 30.10.1988.

## TRADE UNIONS

**Out of 83 General Secretaries of trade unions, only five were women.**

Source: TUC, January 1989.

## MILITARY

Women do not have the option to fight and are largely restricted to the lowest levels of power in the armed forces.

## PRIESTS

**There are still no women priests** in either the Anglican or Catholic Churches in the UK although there are ordained women deacons. The Church of England will not vote again on this issue before 1991 and possibly later.

# SEXUAL DISCRIMINATION

## CHILDCARE

## Only 15% of mothers work full-time

Childcare is now probably the major obstacle to mothers working and pursuing a career:

- **'having children can cost a woman up to half her potential lifetime's earnings whereas men's employment experience and earnings are largely unaffected by fatherhood'** (Bronwen Cohen);
- a mother of two still takes on average seven years out of the labour force.

Having children may lead to a drop on the ladder of status as well as lost time — over two-thirds of working mothers of children under 10 are part-timers, and 45% of them return to a lower job than they had before motherhood. Women's pensions are also adversely affected by motherhood.

There is increasing agreement that women receive too little help with childcare and inadequate rewards for motherhood and housework generally. Among the remedies proposed are increased childcare facilities, tax relief for childcare, crèches at work and paternity leave legislation.

The Home Office published a childcare charter in April 1989, which included a variety of proposals to improve childcare, such as encouraging employers to use the tax relief available for childcare facilities and schools to use their facilities for after-school and holiday play schemes.

Source: Bronwen Cohen, Caring For Children, Commission of the European Communities 1988.

## Working mothers

Of mothers with dependent children in 1984 aged 16-59, only 15% worked full-time, and only 33% worked part-time. The younger their children, the fewer the mothers who work — only 4% of mothers with a child under the age of 2 worked full-time.

Source: General Household Survey 1984.

## Daycare and education

There were school places for only 47.6% of children aged 3 and 4 in the UK in 1987, and daycare places for only 19.3% of all under-5s in 1986. While there have been considerable improvements in our provision of school and daycare places for under-5's, we are still far behind many other countries.

Sources: Social Trends 1989; Regional Trends 1988.

## Housework

Wives still do most housework, according to research by Grey's advertising agency in 1988. They do 80% of the washing and ironing, and 60% of the cleaning and cooking.

But 80% of women were reported to be satisfied with that arrangement, although 75% of mothers also feel that motherhood is undervalued. (These results were largely echoed by another study for the DMB&B advertising agency.)

Source: Times, 31.8.88.

## Value

**One estimate values women's work as mothers and housewives at 25-40% of the GNP of industrialised countries.** Another puts it at one-third of the world's economic product.

Source: Joni Seager and Ann Olson, Women in the World 1986.

# RACIAL DISCRIMINATION

The Runnymede Trust report, Different Worlds, found extensive racial discrimination in all the main spheres of British life — jobs, housing, education, immigration control, the health service, enforcement of law and order, and racial depictions in the media. Some of this discrimination is too subtle to be quantified. The Runnymede report argues that the way ethnic minorities are considered and labelled as a problem in every sphere of life is itself an act of discrimination.

The ethnic population stands at 2,432,000 (4.5% of the general population). This was the estimated total for the ethnic minorities, 1984-86. They are more concentrated among under-16s, amounting to 7.5% of the population.

Source: OPCS, Labour Force Survey.

## Unemployment

**Unemployment among ethnic groups was DOUBLE that among the white population** in 1984-86, 20% compared with 10%.

The difference was even starker for males of ethnic minorities aged 25-44, with the highest qualifications (including degrees) — 9% were unemployed, compared with only 3% of whites.

The Race and Immigration report by the Runnymede Trust found that discrimination, direct and indirect, was the most important factor in high racial unemployment. Language problems were a factor too, but language was often used as an excuse for discrimination.

Source: Race and Immigration, Runnymede Trust Bulletin, no. 159, September 1983.

## Job discrimination

**One in three employers discriminate against black job applicants** according to the Runnymede Trust. So there must be at least tens of thousands of acts of racial discrimination in job recruitment in Britain each year. Michael Day, chairman of the Commission for Racial Equality,

has warned that the UK is in danger of creating 'a black underclass who become trapped, despairing and alienated from the rest of the community'.

Source: speech to Howard League for Penal Reform, 14.9.88.

## Case study

Researchers had identically qualified Afro-Caribbeans, Asians and whites apply in writing and by phone for the same sorts of jobs in London, Manchester, and Birmingham, including positions as sales representatives, secretaries, clerks, office juniors and skilled manual workers. In 38% of cases, the white applicant was interviewed while the blacks were refused. The overall level of discrimination was much the same for Asians and Afro-Caribbeans, black men and women, and for each geographical area.

## Occupations

Ethnic groups were more likely to be in manual occupations — 78% of West Indian/Guyanese and 64% of Pakistani/Bangladeshi males compared with only 54% of white males (though the figure for Indian males was 45%). 42% of working women in ethnic minorities were manually employed, as against only 35% of white women. Black men were almost four times as likely as white men to be working in the hotel and catering industry, which is well known for its low wages and poor working conditions.

Source: Alan Walker and Carol Walker, The Growing Divide, Child Poverty Action Group 1987.

# RACIAL DISCRIMINATION

**Seventeen-year-old Richard Grant Stokes, first black man to graduate to exclusive ranks of the Household Division in recent years (July, 1987)**

## Education

The Swann Report found that while Asian children's achievement at school is close to that of white children, West Indian children are under-achieving at school, and Bangladeshis are seriously under-achieving.

It also found that racial discrimination both inside and outside education was largely to blame (IQ was *not* a significant factor). 'Intolerant' teachers spend more time first with white boys, then with Asian boys, and less with Asian girls and West Indian boys. Black pupils receive much less teacher time than other groups, and are often placed on courses or entered for exams at levels below their abilities and ambitions.

Source: Education for All, The Report of the Committee of Inquiry into the Education of Children from Ethnic Minority Groups (1985) (The Swann Report), London.

## Housing

**Ownership.**   While more Asians (72%) are home owners than whites (59%) or Afro-Caribbeans (41%), their homes are usually in less desirable city areas and are overcrowded.

**60% of Bangladeshi, 47% of Pakistani, and 3% of white households are classified as overcrowded.**

**Allocation.**   Various reports on local authorities such as Liverpool, Hackney and Tower Hamlets have shown that their housing departments discriminate against black people in practice, though not in principle, allocating them inferior housing to white people.

**Racial harassment.**   Various reports in 1987 showed that there is extensive racial harassment in housing. The Newham Crime Survey found that **one in four black residents had been a victim of some form of racial harassment in the last year.**

Source: New Year 1988, Another Disastrous Year for London's Homeless, London Housing Unit, 31 December 1987.

SOURCE: Paul Gordon and Anne Newnham, Different Worlds, Runnymede Trust, September 1986.

# ANTI-GAY DISCRIMINATION

**The 'age of consent' for gay men is 21**

Arson attack on gay homes and clubs

BY MARGARET ROOKE

**ESTHER RANTZEN'S GREAT CRUSADE** SEE PAGE 8

## DAILY EXPRESS

Wednesday November 5 1986   20p   ***

THE VOICE OF BRITAIN

**THE Sun**

lay, May 6, 1986   18p   TODAY'S TV IS ON PAGE 12

**£0,000 BINGO!**

y's lucky numbers   See Page 25

EXCLUSIVE : Left accused of wanting a homosexual to be appointed in every school

Gillespie : " Lies "

# PARENT FURY OVER GAY TEACHERS

ANGRY parents last night accused an extremist council of planning to put a homosexual teacher in every one of its schools.

And they claimed "a militant gang " of councillors want the teachers to wear a badge declaring, " I'm gay."

ne head in the troubled Lond ough of Haringey said the eme as " utter n

**THE WRECKING OF OUR SCHOOLS — Pages 18, 27**

By DANIEL McGRORY

The militant Labour regime led by controversial Bernie Grant about employing m

members of The Par met the cha jobs.

5   ***

# VILE BOOK IN SCHOOL

**Pupils see**

Perverted . . . a page from the book showing Jenny

ctober 18 1985

**LOOK AT POP IN THE EXPRESS**

**DISCOVER DALTRY'S NEW ROLE: CENTRE PAGES**

# Gay sex lessons on Loony Left's rates

Hard-up council offers staff tips on homosexuality

TOWN HALL staff will get the chance to go on sex courses to ask themselves the crucial question : Should I be gay?

Loony Lambeth Council, a hard-up, Left-wing, South London borough, is setting up lessons — on the rates — about the homosexual birds and bees at a cost of £600 a time.

A report backing the scheme says : "Heterosexism is one form of discrimination which is not regarded as being separate from other forms of discrimination." Course students will be urged to "challenge their own heterosexism."

And they will be encouraged to "re-examine the ways in which they have learned to be heterosexual."

The problems of coloured homosexuals, who suffer " double discrimination " will not be forgotten.

Nor will disabled people be left out. The report says : " Training is intended to challenge other forms of discrimination, such as ablebodyism."

Borough staff and councillors are to be offered the choice of two courses, two

By DON COOLICAN
Home Affairs Editor

days for £601 per person, or a concentrated £360 single day.

The lessons, still to be rubber-stamped by the full Lambeth council, have been planned by the groups LAGER (Lesbians and Gays Employment Rights) and WHAT (Women's Hetero-sexual Awareness Trainers).

A (male) spokesperson for Lambeth said last night the groups were NOT joke organisations."

But Opposition Tory leader Mrs Mary Leigh said she would be tempted to laugh if she were not so angry.

"The way Lambeth Labour leaders spend ratepayers' cash never ceases to amaze me," she said.

George Gale : Page 9

**Plot case demo**

SIKHS staged a noisy demonstration outside a Leicester court yesterday when four men accused of plotting to murder Indian Prime Minister Rajiv Gandhi were remanded.

e colleagues thought they would catch AIDS. Many in the gay com-munity believe queer bashing' is not on the in-crease but AIDS is in-creasingly the excuse given by their attackers. But Dorian Jabri of the Gay London Police Moni-toring Group believes there has been a massive increase in attacks on gay men recently.

• Tory Right-wing MP Harvey Proctor faces deselection at the end of this month by his Billeri-cay constituency after alle-gations about his private life.

# ANTI-GAY DISCRIMINATION

Gay men and lesbians experience discrimination particularly in the areas of employment, housing, the media and, of course, sexuality. Statistics on that discrimination, though, are hard to come by — and that is arguably another area of discrimination, in this case by the authorities. The police, for example, do not compile statistics on anti-gay violence, although it is widespread in certain areas.

## Employment

A 1985 survey of 195 gay men (80% under the age of 36) found that 6% had been sacked for being gay, and 78% did not state they were gay when last applying for a job.

A 1985 survey of 171 lesbians, (96% under 40) revealed that 7% had been sacked for being lesbian, 12% had received dismissal threats, and 17% felt they had been refused a job for being lesbian.

Such surveys, according to MP Chris Smith, reveal 'the fear, anxiety, and self-protective shell that gay men and lesbians are so often forced to adopt in a hostile world'. LAGER (Lesbian and Gay Employment Rights) argues that under present employment law gay men and lesbians can still be sacked, demoted or refused promotion simply because they are lesbian or gay, and that the law should therefore be changed to make discrimination on the grounds of sexual preference illegal.

Sources: survey, Phil Greasley, Men At Work, LAGER 1986; ed. Nina Taylor, All In A Day's Work, Lesbian Employment Rights 1986.

## Sexuality

Two 19-year-old men were convicted of 'disorderly behaviour' under Section 5 of the 1986 Public Order Act for kissing in public, in Villiers Street in London, on the grounds that their action had caused 'harassment, alarm or distress' to policemen. LAGER complains that this piece of legislation, intended for use against hooligans, has become a means of discriminating against gay men and lesbians.

## Media

The notorious Section 28 of the Local Government Act bans the 'promotion of homosexuality' by local authorities. The NCCL points out that the Government rejected this measure as 'unnecessary and open to harmful misinterpretation' a year before passing it, and fears that it may be used as a tool of discrimination. Examples would be to deny funding to gay clubs and licences to gay social events, or even to stop lesbians and gays using council premises. At the same time, legal opinions received by the NCCL make it clear that such discriminatory actions would be an abuse of Section 28.

## Housing

According to the London Housing Unit, although there is no statistical breakdown on who the single homeless are, it is widely-known that many lesbians become homeless as a direct result of discrimination.

Source: New Year 1988, Another Disastrous Year for London's Homeless, London Housing Unit, 31 December 1987.

# AGEISM

## 88.5%
## of job ads in one survey specified an upper age limit of 40

The above survey by recruitment agency MSL, based on a sample of 928 job ads, provides a frightening example of how difficult it can be for older people to find work. Peter Naylor, deputy chairman of the Institute of Personnel Management and a leading researcher in the field, acknowledges that there is widespread discrimination in industry and the employment sector against older people. He says that headhunters and recruitment agencies specify age in half their recruitment advertisements, although company personnel managers specify age in just 17% of their advertisements. In addition, both men and women civil servants have to retire at 60.

Some employers are changing their attitudes. Tesco's, for example, actively sought 55-65-year-olds when they found they could not fill vacancies for a new store in Crawley, and were very pleased with the results. Nigel Lawson indirectly helped pensioners who want to work in the March 1989 budget — he abolished the 'earnings rule', so that they can now earn as much money as they like without money being docked from their pension. The changing demographics of the 1990s, when there will be a shortfall of young recruits to the labour force, should further help employment for middle-aged and older people. There is even talk of a grey revolution.

## Solutions
In the USA, age discrimination in job ads is illegal.

Robert Rose, chairman of the Association for Retired Persons, has called for a British law comparable to that in the USA, which specifies that an employee cannot be compulsorily retired on the grounds of age.

Sources: survey, Discrimination Against The Over-40s, MSL 1989; The Times, 26.5.1989.

**Police line-up in Wapping during News International dispute**

# CIVIL LIBERTIES

A variety of restrictions have been placed on civil liberties in recent years attracting a great deal of criticism. The powers of government and the authorities have been extended at the expense of the press, media, and the private citizen. As a result, Ronald Dworkin, University Professor of Jurisprudence at Oxford University, and

Professor of Law at New York University, has declared that 'Liberty is ill in Britain'.

The government may retort that on the one hand some liberties have been extended, and on the other, some restrictions, albeit undesirable, have been necessary in the fight against terrorism, particularly in Northern Ireland.

## POLITICAL RIGHTS

### MI5's powers

'No entry on, or interference with property shall be unlawful if it is authorised by a warrant issued by the Secretary of State.'

Official Secrets Act

In other words, under the new Act, MI5 will have the right to burgle homes in pursuit of those who 'undermine democracy by political [or] industrial means', and for the protection of Britain's 'economic well-being' against foreigners — and Parliament will have no right to supervise MI5.

Those who have been victimised by the security service will be allowed to complain to a special tribunal of five lawyers, and a Senior Commissioner, appointed by the Home Secretary and Prime Minister respectively. But victims will have no right to make the results public or to take action in court and may never discover — since it is an offence for journalists to disclose MI5 activities — that they *are* victims anyway. This has therefore been called a Catch-22 law. One victim was Jack Jones, the former trade union leader. MI5 files falsely accused him of being a Soviet agent and were used as advice to ministers to prevent him getting government jobs between 1965 and 1985.

Source: David Leigh, The Wilson Plot 1989.

### Right to protest

Organisers of demonstrations must inform the police one week in advance, unless really impracticable — and that is up to the police to decide.

1986 Public Order Act

The new Public Order Act has given the police much increased powers over marches. They can set conditions in order to prevent serious disorder, damage to property, disruption to the life of the community, or intimidation of others. The Act was first used to prosecute anti-apartheid demonstrators outside South Africa House who had disobeyed an order to move away from what they considered the meaningful position for their protest.

The Act makes it illegal to be 'abusive' or 'insulting' on marches, irrespective of whether anyone is the victim of the abuse or insults. When one of a group of demonstrators walking past Downing Street swore and made V-signs at No. 10, he was arrested and convicted for insulting behaviour.

Source: Index on Censorship, September 1988.

## Voting system

In 1983 25% of the electorate, voting for the Liberal-SDP Alliance, were only able to secure 3.5% of parliamentary seats. In 1987, 22.5%, voting again for the Alliance, could only secure 3.4% of seats.

This is not a new restriction but our current, 'first-past-the-post' voting system is clearly not as democratic as proportional representation, and, as the 1983 and 1987 elections showed, can lead to extremely undemocratic results. On the other hand, some will argue that it is a price worth paying otherwise a very small party, which holds the balance of power, may wield unduly great influence. Those whose votes counted for so little in 1983, and again in 1987, may not be so sure.

## Number of MPs elected

|  | June 1983 | June 1987 |
|---|---|---|
| Conservative | 396 | 375 |
| Labour | 209 | 229 |
| Liberal | 17 | 17 |
| SDP | 6 | 5 |
| SNP | 2 | 3 |
| Plaid Cymru | 2 | 3 |
| Other | 18 | 18 |

## Votes cast — 1983 General Election

|  | Number of votes | % of votes cast | % of seats |
|---|---|---|---|
| Conservative | 13.01 million | 42.4 | 61 |
| Labour | 8.46 million | 27.6 | 32 |
| Liberal | 4.21 million | 13.7 | 2.6 |
| SDP | 3.57 million | 11.6 | 0.9 |

# CIVIL LIBERTIES

## LEGAL RIGHTS

### Detention

**Suspects can be held without being taken before a judge for up to seven days.**

Prevention of Terrorism Act

An appeal against this Act led to the European Court of Human Rights ruling in 1988 that it contravened the European Convention on Human Rights signed by us in 1950, and Britain could not hold people for longer than four days.

The British government has declared that it may derogate from the Convention. It acknowledges that the Prevention of Terrorism Act is an undesirable encroachment on the freedom of citizens, but argues that the Act is needed to fight terrorism. The NCCL argues that this Act would be condemned if operated in any dictatorship:

'**Statistics support the view that this power is often used merely to obtain information**: since 1974, for instance, 6,430 people have been detained under the Prevention of Terrorism Act in Britain on suspicion of involvement in terrorism connected with Northern Ireland. **Of these, only 8.5% were ever charged with any offences.**'

Source: Statement by the Fédération Internationale des Droits de l'Homme, to the 44th Session of the UN Commission on Human Rights, 1 February–11 March 1989

### Diplock courts

In Northern Ireland, the jury system was suspended in 1973 for certain scheduled offences, including criminal and terrorist offences. It was replaced by Diplock courts, where a single judge tries and passes verdict on a case.

### Trials

**If the accused remains silent in court in Northern Ireland, the court may now draw inferences from that action.**

Criminal Evidence (Northern Ireland) Order 1988

The right for an accused person to remain silent without any inferences being drawn has been regarded as a sacred legal right for centuries. At the end of 1988, the government removed this privilege from those in Northern Ireland and simultaneously indicated its intention to press ahead with similar changes for England and Wales. Inferences may now be drawn if the accused maintains silence.

The government will acknowledge that this, along with other measures, is an undesirable encroachment on the freedom of citizens, but argues that such measures are necessary to fight terrorism. The NCCL argues that they will not help the fight and will tend to put defendants in the position of having to prove their innocence.

## PRIVACY

### Access to personal files

Under the Data Protection Act, people have a right to see any computer files held on them by any organisation, apart from those whose disclosure might endanger national security. But the cost can be prohibitive. Data users may charge up to £10 for each request for a file. **To have access to all of the information held by the Metropolitan Police on you could cost a total of £250.**

The catch to the Data Protection Act is that it only allows access to computer records, not manual records. Many people have discovered that their computer file refers to a manual file for more personal and sensitive information — which they still cannot obtain.

SOURCE: NCCL.

# CIVIL LIBERTIES

## FREEDOM OF INFORMATION

## Official secrets

It is against the law for civil servants to reveal matters relating to defence, international relations, security and intelligence. Those who do so will no longer be allowed to plead that it is in the public interest.

*Official Secrets Act*

The new Official Secrets Act will get rid of some of the secrecy which has surrounded government activities throughout this century. Most government activities in principle were secret — even the menu in a department's canteen. Now it will only be those matters relating to defence, international relations, security and intelligence.

But in many respects the Act will intensify secrecy. In the past, officials who revealed secrets could plead that their actions were in the public interest — as Clive Ponting did, successfully, when tried for leaking information about the sinking of the Belgrano in the 1982 Falklands War. Now that defence is invalid. Edward Heath, one of the many critics, has pointed out that under this Act, Duncan Sandys would not have been able in the 1930s to expose the inadequacy of British defences, and the senior civil servant who gave information of a similar kind to Winston Churchill would have been jailed.

Source: Hansard 21.12.88.

## Press sources

The House of Lords ruled that a journalist for the Independent should reveal his confidential sources or face punishment.

This will mean that people will be more reluctant to disclose information to journalists, which should be published in the public interest.

## Confidential material

The police have new powers of seizure. They can, with a court order, force the media, including journalists and photographers, to hand over their confidential, journalistic material such as notebooks, tapes or photos which have never been published.

*Police and Criminal Evidence Act, 1984*

Like the ruling on sources, this will make it even more difficult for journalists to obtain information, and it may mean that journalists and photographers covering riots and demonstrations will be perceived as police agents and thus risk injury.

## Interviews with terrorist supporters

The Home Secretary announced a ban on media interviews with representatives or supporters of Sinn Fein, Republican Sinn Fein, and the Ulster Defence Association on 19 October 1988, prompting comparisons of the United Kingdom with South Africa. In fact, the South African Minister of Justice later cited this act to support his government's own policies of repression and censorship.

One consequence was that the Independent Broadcasting Authority issued a circular to all independent radio stations instructing them not to play a song by the Pogues, which supported pleas of innocence by the Birmingham Six and the Guildford Four, two groups jailed separately for pub bombings in England in 1974. 'This stinks of McCarthyism,' said Pogues manager, Frank Murray.

Source: Observer 20.11.1988.

# PART FIVE
# PUBLIC ORDER

Public disorder may not affect most people directly, but it can affect everyone indirectly. Crime has grown relentlessly over the past two decades, and whether or not it has been exaggerated and overpublicised, the lives of many women and old people in particular have been filled with fear as a result.

Civil conflict though, with the exception of Northern Ireland, has considerably been diminished in the eighties — perhaps too much, some may argue. Industry and business are no longer as fraught with confrontations and strikes as they were in the early eighties and seventies, though whether this is a sign of a more co-operative worker-management relations, or a symptom of a coerced and weaker workforce is open to debate.

# NORTHERN IRELAND

## 93
### killed in sectarian attacks in Northern Ireland (1987)

### 1,130 injured

### 236 explosions and
### 674 shooting incidents

The cold statistics on the civil disturbances in Northern Ireland cannot provide an adequate picture of what it is like to live within those disturbances. The statistics are not even that sensational. There were over three times as many deaths in Washington DC in 1988. But the conflict in Northern Ireland remains one of Britain's greatest and most persistent problems.

## Who?

**Dead.**   Of 93 killed, 66 were civilians and 27 were serviceman. Most of the latter belonged to the Royal Ulster Constabulary — nine to the police, seven to the police reserves. Eight

members of the UDR (Ulster Defence Regiment) were killed, and just three members of the army.

**Injured.**   Civilians accounted for most of the injured, as well as the dead, followed by the RUC. In 1987, they suffered 780 and 246 injuries respectively; in 1986, it was 773 and 622. 92 members of the regular services were injured in 1987.

## Trends

Deaths were 50% up on 1986, and shooting incidents nearly doubled. Most aspects of terrorist activity showed an increase. But the long-term trends seem to be downwards, if erratically. The greatest numbers killed were in 1972, when there were 467 deaths, and in 1976 when there were 297. Altogether there have been over 2,600 deaths connected with the disturbances since 1969.

SOURCE: Northern Ireland Office.

**Milltown Cemetery funeral, March 1988**

# INDUSTRIAL RELATIONS

## 1,920,000 days lost through industrial stoppages (UK, 1986)

The 1980s have seen a relative decline in the loss of working days through industrial stoppages, though trade unionists may argue that this may result from the curbs now placed on union powers, and not necessarily from the absence of any grievance.

However, unofficial action by transport workers brought London to a halt in the spring and summer of 1989, suggesting that the respite from industrial dispute of the mid-1980s may be over, with rising inflation and increasing wage claims placing pressure on management.

### Stoppages
1,074 stoppages were recorded as being in progress in 1986.

### Who?
2,103,000 workers were directly and indirectly involved in stoppages in 1986. Roughly a third of them, 687,000 workers, were involved in stoppages in the heavy industries of metals, engineering, shipbuilding and vehicles.

### How long?
The majority of stoppages were either very short or very long. Roughly a third (369) lasted not more than 5 days, and 19% lasted over 50 days.

### Regions
The North was the region with the highest rate of strikes (2.15 days lost per employee), followed by the North West (1.72 days), and Yorkshire and Humberside (1.4 days).

Source: Regional Trends 1988.

## Union membership
This has fallen steadily from a high of 13.3 million (around 51% of the working population), to 9,240,000 (around a third of the workforce) in 1988.

## Trends
Both the number of strikes and days lost have fallen sharply since the seventies and early eighties. For the period 1976-86, there was an average of 1,693 strikes and 11.1 million days lost a year (an average lifted by the miners' strike in 1984, when a total of 27.1 million days were lost).

SOURCES: Employment Gazette, Department of Employment; Annual Abstract of Statistics 1988.

---

### How Trade Union powers have been curbed in recent years

**The Employment Act 1980**
- limited picketing to the picket's place of work, restricting secondary picketing;
- encouraged secret union ballots, making funds available for that purpose.

**The Employment Act 1982**
- took away trade unions' immunity from civil action;
- removed legal protection from closed shops.

**Trade Union Act 1984**
- made strikes without a ballot illegal

---

# CRIME

## 3,900,000 offences (England and Wales, 1987)

**The real number of crimes committed may be FOUR times greater than those reported.**

Crime is one of Britain's greatest growth industries, having increased almost every year since the 1950s — through both rising and falling unemployment. Although changing figures can sometimes be misleading because of changes in reporting and recording practices, the broad trends have been very stable.

Surprisingly, provisional figures for 1988 offences show a small drop in the overall total, to 3.7 million offences. But little can yet be read into this, and while thefts and burglaries fell in 1988, many more serious crimes like violence against the person and rape are still on the increase.

Sociologists will also point out that white collar crimes, such as fraud, breaches of anti-trust legislation, monopolies, pollution, and embezzlement, are under-reported and under-prosecuted compared with more traditionally blue collar crimes.

## Which crimes?

3.7 million offences (94%) were *crimes against property*
198,900 offences (5%) were *crimes against the person*

### Offences in England and Wales in 1987

| Theft and handling stolen | |
|---|---|
| goods | 2,052,000 (53%) |
| Burglaries | 900,000 (23%) |
| Criminal damage | 589,000 (15%) |
| Violence against the person | 141,000 (3.6%) |
| Sexual offences | 25,200 (0.6%) |
| Rapes | 2,500 (0.06%) |
| Homicides | 635 (0.01%) |
| Fraud and forgery | 130,000 (3.3%) |
| Robberies | 33,000 (0.8%) |

## Real crime

The real total of crimes committed may be four times higher than those recorded by police, including: twice as many burglaries; three to four times as many thefts from vehicles; three to five times as many woundings; twelve times as many offences of vandalism; and fourteen times as many thefts from the person.

Source: 1984 British Crime Survey, Home Office Research Study no. 85.

## Regions

The crime rate is about 80% higher in metropolitan areas than in non-metropolitan areas — 10,400 against 6,200 per 100,000 population. There can be even sharper variations between specific regions — Merseyside and Northumbria with 3,500 burglaries per 100,000 population have nearly *six* times more burglaries than Dyfed-Powys.

There are anomalies. Nottinghamshire and Humberside (rather than London) have the highest recorded rates for both crimes of violence and sexual offences. Differences in police recording practice may partly explain variations.

## Cost of crimes

Crime in Britain is estimated to cost about £15 billion a year in losses by individuals and organisations, and in public spending to tackle the problem.

Source: Costs of Crime, a report by the Crime Prevention Unit 1988.

## Trends

Crime has increased at a remarkably steady rate of about 5-6% a year from 0.5 million offences in the early 1950s. In the 1950s, the average increase was just below 5%, in the 1960s just over 6%, and in the 1970s about 5%. The crime rate has multiplied from 1,000 offences per 100,000 population in the early 1950s, to 7,400 today.

# OFFENDERS

## 536,300
**people found guilty of, or cautioned for, indictable offences (England and Wales, 1987)**

While a great many men (as many as one in three) commit the odd criminal offence at some point in their life, most crime is committed by a small core of offenders. No figures are available about the social class of offenders.

## Who?

**M/F.** Men form the vast majority of offenders. 447,900 (84%) were males. 85,900 (16%) were females. There were 2,500 'other offenders', including companies.

**Age.** Nearly half of all offenders (269,000) were young people under the age of 21. 138,000 were under 17. The worst offenders are male juveniles aged 14 to 17, with a rate of 7,400 offenders per 100,000 population. The rate for males aged 17-21 is also over 7,000, but it drops sharply for males over 21, to 1,280 per 100,000. The peak age for male criminal offenders is 15, as it has been nearly every year since 1975.

Women are catching up in criminality as in other areas. Their highest rate was for 10-to 17-year-olds in Nottinghamshire — 2,100 per 100,000 population.

## Criminal community?

One study which looked at the records of all males born in 1953, showed that **one in three males has been convicted of a standard list offence\* before the age of 28.** However, only 5.5% had been convicted of six or more offences

— and they accounted for 70% of all the group's convictions.

Only 6% of females born in 1953 had been convicted of a standard list offence by the age of 28.

Source: Criminal careers of those born in 1953, 1958 and 1963, Home Office Statistical Bulletin, April 1985.

## Cautioned

Not all offenders are found guilty in court and sentenced. Some, who admit to guilt, are issued with a police caution — a formal warning. In 1987 the figures for indictable offences were 150,000 offenders cautioned, compared to 386,000 offenders found guilty in court.

Offenders are most often cautioned for theft and handling stolen goods (in 38% of such offences) and sexual offences (in 34% of such cases, many of which involved unlawful sexual intercourse between willing partners) and least often cautioned for robbery (5% get a caution).

45% of *females* were cautioned, against 27% of males. *Juveniles* were cautioned more often. 86% of males aged 10-14 and 59% of males aged 14-17 were cautioned, compared to 12% of those over the age of 21.

## Trends

The number of offenders interestingly has NOT increased in proportion to the number of offences. In 1977, for example, there were actually slightly MORE offenders — 537,200. Since then the numbers have moved up and down somewhat erratically between a low of 509,000 (1979) and a high of 589,000 (1985).

Source: Criminal Statistics, England and Wales 1988.

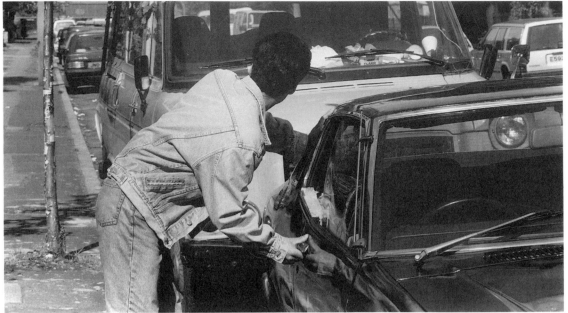

## 2,052,000 thefts (England and Wales, 1987)

We are, as a nation, more given to thieving than any other crime. Theft accounts for **over half of all recorded offences**. We are particularly keen on autocrime (stealing cars and/or their contents) which accounts for over a quarter of all offences.

### What?
Autocrime accounts for half of all theft. In 1987 there were 660,000 thefts from vehicles, and 390,000 thefts (or unauthorised taking) of motor vehicles.

Second and third favourites were shop goods (247,000) and pedal cycles (119,000). 'Theft from the person', including pickpocketing, accounted for a relatively small 34,000 offences.

### Causes
One estimate is that vehicles are *unlocked* in about 20% of autocrime.

### Clear-up rate
Only 25% of thefts of vehicles were cleared up, but, on the other hand, about two-thirds of the value of vehicles stolen was recovered. 94% of those who had items stolen from their vehicles did not recover their property.

Source: Costs of Crime, a report by the Crime Prevention Unit, London, 6.12.88.

### Cost
Thefts from vehicles came to £120 million, thefts of vehicles to £662 million.

Source: Costs of Crime, a report by the Crime Prevention Unit, London: 6.12.88.

### Regions
Northumbria has the highest theft rate of all (6,169 offences per 100,000 population), followed by Greater Manchester (6,015). London comes third with 5,422.

### Trends
Thefts have increased 3% a year on average since 1977, although thefts from vehicles have increased by 120% overall.

# BURGLARIES

## 900,000 burglaries (England and Wales, 1987)

Burglaries are the second most common crime, accounting for nearly a *quarter* of all offences. Provisional figures for 1988 show a small drop, suggesting that an increase in do-it-yourself crime prevention measures, such as fitting strong locks to windows and doors, may be having an effect. According to the police, most burglaries are opportunistic and committed by amateurs, who are apparently discouraged by well-protected homes.

## Where?

In almost half of cases (483,000) people's homes were burgled. 417,000 'other buildings', including offices, business and industrial premises, were also burgled.

## How much?

In 25% of recorded burglaries, the value of property stolen was 'nil' — they may though have involved damage to property or theft or articles of no monetary value. In another 25%, the value of property stolen was under £100.

The *average* value of stolen property was £743 in dwellings, and £615 in other buildings.

**£272 million worth of property was stolen from homes in 1987.**

Source: Costs of Crime, a report by the Crime Prevention Unit, London, 6.12.88.

## Fuel meters

In 1987-88, over 13,000 burglaries referred to Victims Support (out of a total of 237,000 burglary referrals) involved theft from a fuel meter.

Source: National Association of Victims Support Schemes.

## Firearms

were used in under 110 of all 900,000 burglaries in 1987.

## Neighbourhood Watch

There are almost 56,000 Neighbourhood Watch schemes in Britain.

Source: Great Britain 1989.

## Trends

Burglaries have increased at an average rate of 4% since 1977.

### Recovered
87% of burglary victims did *not* recover their property.

Source: Costs of Crime, a report by the Crime Prevention Unit, London, 6.12.1988.

# ROBBERIES

## 33,000 robberies (England and Wales, 1987)

Robberies (which are thefts with the threat of violence) include muggings as well as attacks on shops and banks. While they represent less than 1% of all crime, they have been increasing faster than most offences for a long time. One recent and unpleasant innovation has been the craze for 'steaming', when groups of youths run through a train robbing 25 or more passengers at a time.

### How much?
Most robberies do not result in a grand haul. The value of property stolen was nil in 16% of robberies, and over £1,000 in only 10% of robberies.

### Where?
Most armed robbers preferred softer targets than banks. 25% of robberies take place in shops or stalls, 15% involve highway robberies (including security vans), 14% in building societies, 8% in garages and service stations, and 6% in banks.

### Weapons
Pistols and shotguns were the weapons used in about 75% of armed robberies and most of the more serious offences of violence against the person. The weapons most used in robberies were:

| | |
|---|---|
| Pistols | 1,370 |
| Long-barrelled shotguns | 280 |
| Sawn-off shotguns | 450 |
| Imitation firearms | 201 |

### Regions
London with its wealth of shops and financial institutions was not surprisingly the most robbed region, with 250 offences per 100,000 population. Merseyside was next (116).

### Trends
The average annual increase in robberies between 1977 and 1987 was 9% a year, somewhat higher than overall crime which has been rising at between 5 and 6% a year.

## 9,002 firearms offences (England and Wales, 1987)

We are not a particularly trigger-happy nation. Firearms are used in less than 0.3% of notifiable offences, although this percentage has been increasing fairly steadily since the seventies.

### Weapons
Pistols were used in 1,500 offences (17%); shotguns were used in 1,200 offences (14%); and air weapons were used in 5,200 offences (57%). Pistols and shotguns were the main weapons used in armed robbery and more serious offences of violence against the person. Air weapons were used in over 90% of less serious offences of violence against the person or criminal damage.

### Ownership
There were 159,000 firearm certificates in England and Wales in 1987, and 861,000 shotgun certificates.

### Trends
Firearm offences are down from the high of 9,742 in 1985, but the broad trend is up — from only 2,070 in 1972.

SOURCE: Social Trends 1988.

**Police gunmen at bank raid, in Preston, September 1988**

# FRAUD AND FORGERY

**Businessman Peter Clowes at Guildhall magistrates' court, after Barlow-Clowes financial empire collapsed, December 1988**

## 133,000 offences (England and Wales, 1987)

Fraud and forgery are only 3.5% of all offences. But deciding what constitutes fraud or forgery is often difficult, and the numbers can change considerably in line with recording practice. Much fraud — company fraud, such as computer frauds on banks — may never be reported by victims intent on preserving their reputations, and tax frauds are rarely prosecuted. The commonest frauds are through cheques and credit cards. Major frauds are only a small part of the total.

### Dole fraud vs tax fraud

While tax fraud costs the State far more, Social Security fraud (taking benefits to which one is not entitled) is prosecuted with much more zeal.

**Tax fraud of £5,000 million resulted in 20 prosecutions (1986 figures); dole fraud of £500 million resulted in 14,000 prosecutions.** In fact, there were 500 prosecutions for tax offences in total, but most related to specialist sub-contractor exemption certificate offences — the building lump fraud. There were only 20 prosecutions in 1986 for submitting false returns of income or making false claims for personal allowances.

The Inland Revenue may argue that its softer approach is more effective. In 1987 it recovered £1.7 billion in unpaid tax.

Sources: Inland Revenue; estimates given to the Public Accounts Committee, quoted in the Observer, 23.10.88.

### Company fraud

This includes computer fraud, industrial espionage, bribes and petty pilfering. Insurance payments covering 'white collar crime' (another name for this category of fraud) are only around £78 million a year. But the real cost to British companies is about £1,500 million according to one estimate. Company awareness of such fraud is claimed to be low, and security systems seem to be correspondingly lax.

Source: White Collar Crime in the UK, Saladin Security Systems, London, 9.1.1989.

### Who?

White collar crime is committed, according to the above report, by people with a 'predisposition to steal'. They are often under pressure due to debts.

### Trends

This category of crime has increased by an average 4% every year since 1980.

# CRIMINAL DAMAGE

## 589,000
## incidents of criminal damage
## (England and Wales, 1987)

Criminal damage includes vandalism and damage to our cities — vandalised doors in blocks of flats, broken phone boxes, smashed up bus shelters, damaged trees or shrubs. **The British Crime Survey suggests that less than 10% of actual offences are reported** — although even so they account for 15% of all recorded offences. A great percentage are committed by young people.

## Costs
The annual cost to individual victims of criminal damage has been put at £100 million, and to local authorities at £500 million. At the same time, of the total 589,000 offences in 1987, 175,500 resulted in damage of £20 or under.

Sources: Costs of Crime, Crime Prevention Unit, London, 6.12.1988; Home Office.

## Arson
In 1987, 18,900 cases of arson were recorded. *Half* of all large fires are started *deliberately*. The *cost* of arson is put at more than £300 million a year.

Source: report on arson to the Standing Conference on Crime Prevention, 6.12.88.

## Firearms
were used in 3,453 offences of criminal damage.

## Regions
The rate of criminal damage is higher in Greater Manchester than in any other area, with 2,129 offences per 100,000 population, followed by Northumbria with 1,639, and London and Merseyside very close behind.

## Trends
Long-term, criminal damage has been increasing sharply. The 589,000 offences in 1987, while only slightly up on 1986, are sharply up from 1980's 360,000 offences.

# VIOLENCE AGAINST THE PERSON

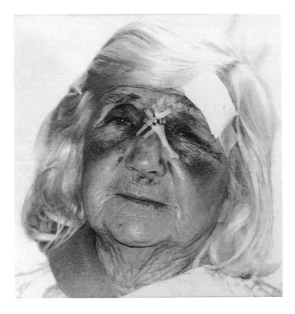

**An 86-year-old pensioner, mugged in Bristol (1987)**

## 141,000
**offences of violence against the person (England and Wales, 1987)**

## 7,900
**wounding offences (or other acts endangering life)**

This category includes murder; attempted murder; threats and manslaughter; wounding, and malicious wounding; cruelty to, or neglect of, children; assault; and hooliganism. In fact, the 1988 figure is expected to be up another 20,000 to over 160,000 offences.

The figures certainly bear out the depiction of Britain in the media as an increasingly violent and hooligan country. One worrying trend is the spread of violence, particularly drunken brawls and riots, to the rural areas of England and Wales. The Chief Constable of Surrey, Brian Hayes, has spoken of an 'alarming picture of nationwide disorder'. His report, Public Disorder Outside Metropolitan Areas, found that police had difficulty in getting reinforcements to the scene in good time in 251 violent and group disorder incidents in 1987. Of these, 75 were in small towns, 29 in villages, and 33 in seaside towns.

### Football hooligans
In 1988, there were 6,147 arrests at football league matches and 6,542 spectators were expelled from grounds (though not all the arrests led to convictions and not all were inside the grounds).
Source: Hansard 17.1.89.

### Racist/anti-gay violence
Organisations for both racial and gay rights are extremely concerned that police start recording offences of anti-racial and anti-gay violence as such, so that the seriousness of both problems can be measured and assessed.

### Regions
The most violent region was Nottinghamshire with 602 offences per 100,000 population, then Humberside with 583. London, i.e. the Metropolitan Police District, comes considerably down the list with 312.

### Trends
Before sharp jumps in both 1987 and 1988, crimes of violence rose steadily but undramatically from 97,000 offences in 1980.

# DOMESTIC VIOLENCE

## 500,000
## women are attacked in their homes each year in England and Wales

The above estimate comes from a Home Office report surveying all the literature on violence against women. It can only be a crude estimate since it is difficult to get precise statistics on domestic violence. But there can be no doubt that such violence is very widespread. It ranges from slaps and punches to stories such as: 'I have had a knife stuck through my stomach. I have had a poker put through my face. I have no teeth where he knocked them all out. I have been burnt with red hot pokers. I have been sprayed with petrol and stood there while he flicked lighted matches at me. . . .'

Remedies suggested by the Home Office report include, in the short term, strong law enforcement by the police and, in the long term, raising community awareness of the problem.

### When?
Domestic violence occurs most often at night and on weekends or holidays.

### Why?
The main sources of violence were possessiveness and jealousy, demands concerning labour and services, and money.

### Regions
In London over 1,000 women a week phone the police about domestic violence. The police regard it as 'a very serious problem'. In a 1986 survey of Islington, there were 2,500 cases of domestic violence in one year. In one Yorkshire community surveyed, 60% of the 129 women

interviewed reported some form of 'threatening, violent or sexually harassing behaviour'.

SOURCES: Police Response to Domestic Violence, Briefing Paper no. 1, Police Monitoring and Research Group 1986; Jones, Maclean and Young, Islington Crime Survey 1986; Domestic Violence: An Overview of the Literature, HMSO 1989; London Women's Aid.

# HOMICIDES

## 635 homicides (England and Wales, 1987)

'Homicide' covers murder, manslaughter and infanticide, but not all offences where a death occurs, e.g. causing death by reckless driving. (In 1987 there were 292 such driving offences.) In reality, homicides tend to be more domestic than the gun-filled myths that dominate our TV and cinema screens. They are also very rare events, even if on the rise.

## How?

The most common tools and methods of murder in 1987 were: using a sharp instrument (33%), hitting and kicking (16%), strangulation (15%), blunt instrument (13%), shooting (13%). Shooting was unusually high in 1987 because of the massacre at Hungerford, when Michael Ryan killed 16 people. Shooting only accounted for an average of about 8% of homicides between 1977 and 1986.

## Whom?

**Relation.**   The victim was acquainted with the killer in the majority of cases — 64% in 1987, and, even more, 73% on average for 1977-86. In 24% of cases, the victim was a friend or acquaintance; in 37%, either family or a lover or former lover. 10% of victims were either son or daughter of the killer, 16% were the spouse or cohabitant, present or past.

**M/F.**   A little over 60% of victims in 1987 were men, although the sex ratio has occasionally been even in the past.

**Age.**   Victims can be all ages. The most at-risk group are infants under 1 year. The next two are men aged 16-30, and men aged 30-50.

**Police.**   Few police officers are killed — there were three in 1987, (one in the Hungerford incident) and a total of 24 for 1977-87.

## Why?

The main, apparent reasons for homicide were 'quarrel, revenge or loss of temper' (49% of cases), and 'In furtherance of theft or gain' (10% of cases). Both percentages have been fairly constant over the years. Interestingly, acts of terrorism, gang warfare, feud or faction fighting (which probably account for most TV and screen deaths), only produced 13 homicides in 1987 — 2% of cases.

---

### Does the death penalty deter?

According to an Amnesty report which both reviewed studies of the death penalty worldwide and conducted research of its own, there is no statistical evidence that the death penalty acts as a deterrent. Roughly 40% of countries do not use the death penalty.

Source: report, When The State Kills, Amnesty 1988.

---

## International comparison

While our figures are serious enough, the UK is a very peaceful nation compared with the USA where over 20,000 people die every year from gunfire.

## Trends

The general trend over the last 10 years has been upwards from 418 offences in 1977, to 635 in 1987 (England and Wales), but there have been occasional falls.

SOURCE: Criminal Statistics, England and Wales, 1987.

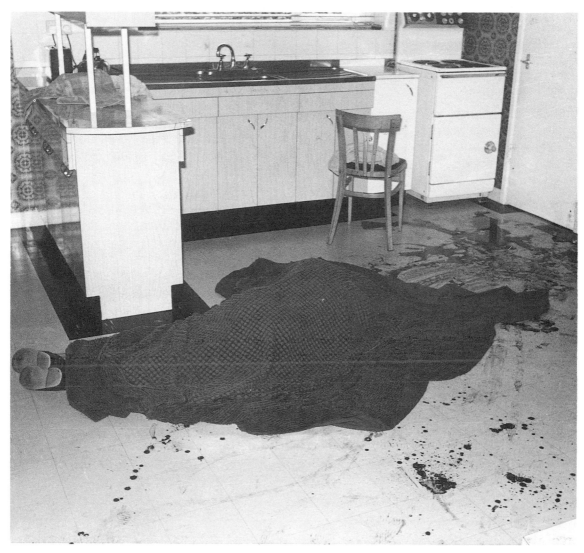

**One of Michael Ryan's victims in Hungerford, August 1987**

# CHILD SEXUAL ABUSE

## 7,119
## victims of sexual abuse
## (England and Wales, 1987)

Child sexual abuse captured the headlines in 1987, with the notorious Cleveland affair in which a local authority separated scores of parents and children. One of the key official figures, Dr Marietta Higgs, is reported to have believed that about one in 10 children were affected. A MORI poll in 1988 seemed to vindicate her, revealing that about one in 12 adults had been sexually abused before the age of 16 (and a 1984 MORI poll was roughly in line with a figure of 10%). On further examination, that abuse encompassed a wide spectrum of activities. 11% of those 'sexually abused', i.e. roughly one in 110 of all questioned, had actually had intercourse.

The NSPCC's estimates show less child sexual abuse — they are based on the registers they keep of local authorities, embracing about 10% of the child population. But the NSPCC acknowledge that actual sexual abuse far exceeds that which is recorded.

### Definition
According to the NSPCC, sexual abuse is 'the involvement of . . . children in sexual activities they do not truly comprehend, to which they are unable to give informed consent or that violates the taboos of social life'.

These are some of the activities quoted by MORI interviewees, along with the percentages who were subjected to them:

- indecent exposure                                26%
- shown pornography                                12%
- touched in a sensual way
  (but not on sexual organs)                       41%
- asked to do something intimate                   21%
- kissed                                            9%
- sexual intercourse                               11%

## Abused

**M/F.** Young girls account for 83% of victims, according to an NSPCC estimate.

**Age.** The average age of children on NSPCC registers was 10 years and 2 months in 1986. But children of all ages are at risk — the NSPCC found that 18% of their subjects were under 4, and they have even dealt with infants under 12 months.

## Abusers

**Relation.** The abusers are usually part of the family: fathers, stepfathers or father substitutes in 60% of cases, brothers or other relatives in 20%, and mothers or substitutes in less than 2% of cases.

**Class.** All social classes can be implicated, but abuse seems more common in the poorer sections of the community. NSPCC register research showed that only 19% of mothers and 35% of fathers were in paid employment, and 10% of mothers/substitutes and 34.5% of fathers had criminal records. Nearly 40% of families had four or more children.

## Effects
The effects can vary enormously. A few children are left unaffected, others can have nightmares and be scarred for life. According to the MORI poll, 13% of those abused as children believed they had suffered permanently damaging effects. 72% believed it had no long-term effects (although 62% found it either 'very disturbing' or 'unpleasant at the time'). 9% believed it had actually *improved* the quality of their lives.

That 13% figure, small as it might seem, would mean that more than 322,000 people in England and Wales have been seriously affected.

# CHILD PHYSICAL ABUSE

## Trends

Child sexual abuse is increasing, and younger children are being affected, according to NSPCC research — but this has only been covering numbers large enough to arrive at nationally valid estimates since 1985.

SOURCES: NSPCC; survey of 15-24-year-olds in the London area, Young People, MORI Poll, 3.5.88; Child Abuse, MORI Poll, September 1984.

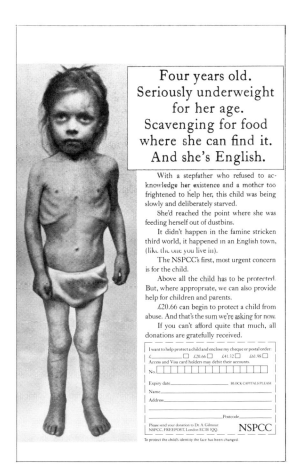

Four years old.
Seriously underweight
for her age.
Scavenging for food
where she can find it.
And she's English.

With a stepfather who refused to acknowledge her existence and a mother too frightened to help her, this child was being slowly and deliberately starved.

She'd reached the point where she was feeding herself out of dustbins.

It didn't happen in the famine stricken third world, it happened in an English town, (like the one you live in).

The NSPCC's first, most urgent concern is for the child.

Above all the child has to be protected. But, where appropriate, we can also provide help for children and parents.

£20.66 can begin to protect a child from abuse. And that's the sum we're asking for now.

If you can't afford quite that much, all donations are gratefully received.

**NSPCC campaign literature**

## 8,044 victims (England and Wales, 1987)

This estimate, based on the NSPCC Register Research, applies purely to physical abuse of children under the age of 17, and not to other recognised categories of abuse, such as physical neglect (e.g. starvation), failure to thrive, and emotional abuse (due to persistent neglect and rejection).

David Mellor, Minister for Health, speaking to an NSPCC conference in November 1988, came up with the first all-embracing figure for child abuse victims in this country. It was only a stab, as a belated response to the entreaties of organisations like the NSPCC for some official statistics, and came to: **39,300 children on Child Protection Registers**.

This actually corresponds roughly with the NSPCC figure once all the other categories of abuse are taken into account, as well as the large number of children considered 'at risk' but not actually abused, e.g. the brother or sister of a child who has had his arm broken.

## How bad?

Of over 8,000 abused children, there were according to NSPCC estimates 1% fatally injured, 13% seriously injured, and 86% suffering moderate injuries such as bruising.

SOURCE: NSPCC.

# SEX OFFENCES

## 25,200
## sexual offences (England and Wales, 1987)

### Which crimes?
'Sexual offences' include crimes such as rape, indecent assault, unlawful sexual intercourse with a girl under 13 or 16, procuration, incest, bigamy and gross indecency with a child.

### Regions
Nottinghamshire and Humberside have the highest and second highest rates not only of violence but also of sexual offences, with 104 and 92 offences per 100,000 population respectively. Next comes Gwent with 73. The Metropolitan Police District has 53.

### Trends
Sexual offences in 1987 were 20% higher than 1977, and 11% higher than 1986.

### 'Reclaim The Night'

**67% of women only go out alone after dark when really necessary; 90% are frightened or cautious of going out on their own.**

According to a World in Action survey of January 1988, the overwhelming majority of women are afraid to go out after dark, and their movements are correspondingly restricted. Only 12% of women think men understand their fear.

## 2,471 rapes
## (England and Wales, 1987)
## The real total may exceed
## 10,000

The London Rape Crisis Centre estimates the real total of rapes to be at least four times recorded offences, since only 25% of women who ring them report the offence to the police. Other estimates put the real figure as much as 10 or even 25 times higher. There is no estimate of rape inside marriage (which technically does not exist).

In addition, there were 13,340 reported indecent assaults.

# DRUG OFFENCES

## Rapists

Most rapists are known to the victim. One British study found that among rapists, over 50% had prior contact with the victim; 16% were a friend, lover or relative; and 38% abused their power or position of trust in relation to the victim.

## Where?

Contrary to myth, rape occurs much less in dark streets and parks, than inside buildings and in the victim's own home.

## Rape in marriage

is not a crime. If a man has sex with his wife without her consent, he is not guilty of rape, because the law assumes that 'in marriage she hath given up her body to her husband'. However, a landmark decision in Edinburgh on March 3 1989, means that Scottish husbands can now be charged with raping their wives. Perhaps the same protection may yet be extended to women in England and Wales, as it has been in most Scandinavian countries, the Eastern Bloc and several states in the USA.

Source: The Rape Controversy, NCCL 1988.

## Trends

Rape offences almost doubled between 1983 and 1987, although whether that is due to more rapes, or more women being ready to report them, is difficult to assess. Indecent assaults on women have risen by about 20% in 10 years, from 11,000 in 1977 to over 13,000 in 1987.

## 23,200 found guilty, or cautioned (England and Wales, 1987)

Drug trafficking, consumption and convictions have all risen sharply through the 1980s. Most seizures and convictions relate to lesser drugs like cannabis, but there has been a recent rise in seizures of cocaine, which looks like replacing heroin as the main drug problem.

## Seizures

There were 30,500 drug seizures in 1987:

- Class A drugs: 3,500 seizures including a total of 235 kg of heroin and 407 kg of cocaine.
- Class B drugs: 28,000 seizures including a total of 26,482 kg of cannabis.

## Convictions

Most offences of which people were found guilty — 11,106 — involved 'possession of a controlled drug'. 1,744 offenders were found guilty of 'supplying or offering to supply a controlled drug'.

## Confiscation orders

£1.2 million was paid to the courts in 1987, under the Drug Trafficking Offences Act, 1986. This requires anyone in England and Wales convicted of a drug trafficking offence to pay, on top of any sentence, an amount equal to the proceeds from their trafficking activities.

## Trends

Drug offences have risen steeply from 11,900 in 1979. So too have hauls of cocaine, up from 13.7 kg in 1977 to 407 kg in 1987, and cannabis, up from 14,932 kg in 1977 to nearly twice that in 1987. Heroin seizures, though, have fallen from their 1985 peak of 366 kg.

SOURCES: Social Trends 1989.

# VICTIMS

# CLEAR-UP RATE

## 328,000 victims referred to Victim Support in 1987-88

Criminals often get much more attention than their victims. But hundreds of thousands of crimes mean hundreds of thousands of victims. Even if the crimes do not appear serious — the majority of victims have been burgled — there can be long-lasting after-effects: 'I am awake all night, and every creak is someone downstairs.' 'I still have that hollow feeling when I get home from work and turn the key in the door.' There are also many thousands of victims of assaults, where the damage is physical as well as psychological.

### Who?
The numbers of crime victims referred in 1987-88 to Victim Support (short for the National Association of Victims Support Schemes) included:

| | |
|---|---|
| Burglary in a dwelling | 237,389 |
| Attacks (robbery, wounding, assault) | 42,421 |
| Theft from person | 22,613 |
| Rape | 913 |
| Other sexual offences | 2,937 |
| Homicide | 306 |
| Other | 21,595 |
| Total | 328,174 |

### The Criminal Injuries Compensation Board
introduced in Great Britain in 1964, received **43,054 claims for attacks in 1987-88**, ranging from minor assaults to murder. It paid out £45 million to victims and their families.

But there are criticisms that it settles only 40% of its claims in less than 12 months and that not all its guidelines, which range from £550 for 'an uncomplicated broken nose' to £4,000 for a rape from which a woman 'makes a full recovery', are generous or adequate.

### Case
A man of 23 was beaten and forced to watch his girlfriend's rape, suffering multiple skull fractures, a blood clot on the brain and loss of hearing in one ear. He lost his job and had to live on Social Security. He received a final payment of £3,000.
Source: Sunday Times, 24.7.88.

### Trends
Twenty years ago, the Criminal Injuries Compensation Board received 6,000 claims and paid out £1.6 million, compared to 43,000 and £45 million in 1987-88.
Source: Social Trends 1989.

SOURCE: National Association of Victims Support Schemes, Annual Report 1987-88.

## 33% of crimes are cleared up (England and Wales, 1987)

An offence is 'cleared up' if a person is charged, summonsed or cautioned, or if it is omitted and taken into consideration, or not proceeded with (e.g. when a child under the age of criminal responsibility is involved). The clear-up rate has fallen from 45% in 1971.

### Which offences?
Most serious offences are cleared up, including 97% of homicides, 75% of violence against the person and sexual offences, and 70% of frauds and forgeries. But the rate falls to 30% for theft and burglaries, although here there are wide variations, from 98% for handlign stolen goods to 11% for theft of pedal cycles.

# PRISONERS

## Average prison population: 56,400 (UK, 1987)

As the crime wave has grown, so has the prison population. Some argue that crime (and ultimately the prison population) can only be reduced by stiffer sentences and harsher penalties, others say that we need lesser punishments, more rehabilitation, and more consideration for certain offenders, such as fine defaulters.

There is little argument though that British prisoners are harshly treated — overcrowded and cooped up for too long. The riots that seem to feature regularly in the news come as no surprise. An extensive prison building programme is promised, but if the prison population grows as projected in the 1990s, there may be new strains on the prison service.

## Who?

**M/F.** Only about 2,000 (3%) of the average prison population were women.

**Under 21.** Crime is strongly related to youth — around one in five prisoners were under 21.

**Race.** The ethnic minority communities in England and Wales in 1987 supplied 14.8% of sentenced prisoners, mainly West Indian, Guyanese or of African origin, and 21% of prisoners on remand at 30 June 1987.

**Mentally ill.** A joint DHSS/Home Office working party estimated that there were about 1,500 mentally disordered people in prison on the basis of a census in October 1986.

SOURCE: On the State of the Nation's Health 1987.

## Sentences

**Length.** In 1987, the lengths of sentences for male prisoners, 21 or over, were between 6 months and 4 years for 66% (21,200); over 4 years for 25% (8,180); and Life for 9% (2,854).

**Time served.** Most prisoners do not serve their full sentence. Apart from 'life' prisoners, the average time served by prisoners discharged in 1986 was between 44% (of sentences from one-and-a-half to four years) and 59% (of sentences up to six months). On the whole, the shorter the sentence, the higher proportion is served. Life sentences meant 10 to 11 years in custody on average for adult males first released in 1986 — a fairly constant figure in recent years.

**Remand.** Not all prisoners have been sentenced. On 30 April, 1988, for example, 22% of the average prison population in England and Wales — 10,500 people — were being held on remand, either awaiting trial or convicted and awaiting sentence. Untried male prisoners spent an average of 56 days in custody on remand in 1987, but they can spend up to 18 months inside.

**Variations.** There can be wide variations in sentences between regions — in Essex, for example, 72% of young adults convicted in crown courts are sent to prison (the highest in the country); in Hampshire, it is only 44%.

Source: Teenagers, Prisons and the Courts, Prison Reform Trust 1988.

## Offences

The main offences for male prisoners on 30 June 1987 were:

| | |
|---|---|
| 1. Burglary | 8,904 (23%) |
| 2. Violence against the person | 8,073 (21%) |
| 3. Theft, handling, fraud and forgery | 6,851 (18%) |
| 4. Robbery | 3,765 (10%) |
| 5. Sexual offences | 2,320 ( 6%) |

The order was the same at 30 June 1986.

# PRISONERS

**Fines.**  19,159 were received into prison in 1986 for defaulting on fines for offences, ranging from burglary to prostitution. (In 1983, 520 were imprisoned for failing to pay fines for TV licence evasion.) While their sentences are usually short, under a month, the National Association for the Care and Resettlement of Offenders (NACRO) argues that many offenders are poor (up to 60% are unemployed) and unable to pay the fines in the first place.

Source: NACRO.

**Inmate, Maidstone Prison**

# PRISONERS

## Treatment

**Overcrowding.**   British prisons are notoriously overcrowded. At the worst, in England and Wales in 1987 there were 14,000 sleeping two in a cell, and 5,300 sleeping three in a cell.

The average population exceeded the CNA (certified normal accommodation) of the England and Wales system by 6,450 in 1987 — 49,000 against a CNA of 42,550.

**Punishments.**   Women prisoners are punished for disciplinary offences one-and-a-half times more often as men. In 1987 there were 3.16 punishments per inmate, half of them for offences of 'disobedience or disrespect'. NACRO insists there should be an inquiry.

Source: NACRO.

**Unsanitary.**   The sanitation facilities at Wandsworth Prison, scene of an industrial dispute with prison officers in early 1989, were declared to be in a 'disgraceful state' by the Board of Visitors. Prisoners have to wrap their excrement in paper and throw it out of windows — the parcels are removed in a special skip once a fortnight.

Source: Observer, 5.2.1989.

## Costs

Prison is much more expensive than other penal measures such as community service or probation orders. The average cost of keeping a prisoner in 1987-88 was £275 a week per prisoner, compared with an average of £690 a year per community service order in 1985-86. And community orders only last on average about eight months.

Sources: Report on the Work of the Prison Service, 1987-88, HMSO; Probation Statistics, England and Wales, 1986, HMSO.

## Deterrent?

**Reconvictions.**   Most social scientists acknowledge that prison's value as a deterrent is poor. Of 41,442 males in 1987 **up to 96% new prisoners were reconvictions**. The percentage of new prisoners with *no* previous convictions has long been low, around 5%, though previous conviction information was not recorded on over 25%. 61% had three or more convictions.

Source: Annual Abstract of Statistics 1989.

**68% of male offenders under 21 are reconvictions.** The figures relate to those imprisoned for over three months in 1983, and are much the same for those in detention centres and borstals. They have remained fairly stable over the years as far back as 1975. Stephen Shaw, director of the Prison Reform Trust, has claimed that sending fewer juveniles to prison markedly reduces recidivism.

Source: Guardian, 31.10.1988.

## Trends

Having increased every year since the war except for 1983-84, **the total prison population is projected to reach 63,000-69,000 by 1996**. It was only 40,000 in the mid-70s. There are many more remand prisoners now (over 20% of the average prison population) against 13% in 1978. And they spend longer inside — 57 days for males in 1986 against 29 days in 1977.

Sentences are getting more severe — the average sentence for adult males received from the crown court rose 5% in 1985, 7% in 1986, and looked set for an 8% rise in 1987.

SOURCES: Prison Statistics, England and Wales, 1986; NACRO; Social Trends 1989.

# PART SIX

# ENVIRONMENT

Environment here covers not only the obvious areas of landscape and pollution but also animals. Britain has a poor environmental record, and has become the 'dirty man of Europe' as well as the sick man, notorious for the amount of acid rain we export through the air, the waste we dump in the North Sea, our heavily polluted river water and relatively polluted drinking water.

The government has expressed its conversion to green issues, though many environmental agencies remain cynical about the true level of such a commitment.

# AIR POLLUTION

**Greenpeace billboard in central London during Clean Cars Campaign**

## LEAD EMISSIONS:
## 2,900 tonnes (UK, 1986)

Cars and other vehicles produce 80% of the lead in the atmosphere. Now, it seems, there is an unstoppable drive to convert all our vehicles to lead-free petrol, partly stimulated by the Chancellor's action in making lead-free petrol 10 pence cheaper than 4-star in March 1989, and by advertising campaigns by car manufacturers and petrol suppliers. But Britain has been slow to convert by comparison with many other countries and still has a long way to go.

### Source
Only 3.3 million vehicles could take lead-free petrol in early 1989 (although an estimated 14 million of Britain's 20.5 million cars and light vans could be converted, usually at a cost of about £20). Over 17 million vehicles were still emitting lead.

About 5,000 garages out of 20,000 were selling lead-free petrol in March 1989, compared to none five years previously. Unleaded fuel accounted for only about 5.5% of all petrol sales. But around 250 filling stations were introducing lead-free petrol every week.

Source: Society of Motor Manufacturers and Traders, March 1989; Virginia Bottomley, Minister for Roads and Traffic, March 1989.

### Effects

**The young.** Exposure to lead can cause mental retardation and impair development, and is most damaging to the unborn and the under-8s.

**Food.** 5% of vegetables grown in London have proved unfit for human consumption, according to Dr Robin Russell Jones, chairman of the Campaign for Lead Free Air. 'Everything we touch or eat today is lead contaminated in some way.'

Source: Daily Mail, 3.11.88.

# AIR POLLUTION

## Road tunnels

Sunday Times tests showed the atmosphere in three major road tunnels to be above the EEC's accepted 'safe' level of 2 micrograms of lead per cubic metre of air. They were Rotherhithe (2.17), Queensway (6.7) and Mersey (8.9).

Source: Sunday Times, 13.11.88.

## International comparison

While unleaded petrol made up 5.5% of Britain's petrol sales in early 1989, it made up 52.7% in West Germany, but only 0.75% and 1.3%, respectively, in France and Italy, and 0% in Spain.

Source: Petroleum Industry Association.

## Trends

Britain's lead emissions were down from 6,700 tonnes in 1981, as the result of a two-stage reduction in the permitted lead content of petrol.

# CARBON MONOXIDE EMISSIONS: 5,602,000 tonnes (UK,1986)

Lead is not the only unpleasant and dangerous gas emerging from car exhausts. One solution to the emission of other gases such as carbon monoxide is to fit a catalytic converter — catalysts have been fitted to all new cars in the USA for 15 years. A three-way catalyst can reduce the emission of pollutants from half a ton (as described below) to only 45lb. The British government prefers lean-burn engines, which are cheaper than fitting converters, though not so efficient. A European Parliament decision in April 1989, calling for strict emission controls on new small cars by October 1992, and on other models at slightly different dates, may force the government towards converters.

## Source

The main source of carbon monoxide is road vehicles. The Times had a common car — a 1980 Volkswagen Golf GTI — laboratory-tested and found that over a typical annual mileage of 13,000 miles, the car would produce about *1,056lb* of carbon monoxide, plus 78lb of hydrocarbons and 50lb of nitrogen oxide — just over half a ton of pollutants.

## Effects

Carbon monoxide inhibits the blood absorbing oxygen and can aggravate chronic respiratory and cardiac problems, like angina.

## Trends

Emissions are up from 4,862,000 tonnes in 1976.

# SMOKE EMISSIONS: 270,000 tonnes (UK, 1986)

## Source

Most of our smoke emissions — some 240,000 tonnes — come from domestic coal-burning fires. Smoke produces much of the dirt and grime of industrial towns, but sulphur dioxide is a more serious danger to health.

## Effects

As a result of smoke control programmes, London's winter sunshine has increased by about 50% since 1958.

Source: Great Britain 1989.

## Trends

Smoke emissions have been significantly reduced over the years from 550,000 tonnes in 1971.

# ACID RAIN

**Llanwern Steel Works, Newport, South Wales**

Acid rain occurs when power stations, factories, cars, and other sources burn fossil fuels and release major pollutants such as sulphur dioxide and nitrous dioxides into the air. These combine together and form a deadly cocktail which falls as rain and can damage trees, crops, rivers, streams and wildlife.

Our acid rain affects not only ourselves but also much of Europe, and Britain is now recognised as one of Europe's worst polluters. Ironically, this is partly due to our response to air pollution in the 1950s and the London fogs of 1952 which killed thousands. We built very high factory and power station chimneys, so high that their emissions can be swept right across the North Sea.

Britain originally refused to join the 21 members of the 30 Per Cent Club, formed in 1984, including France, Italy, and Belgium, who agreed to lower their sulphide dioxide emissions by 30 per cent by 1993. Six of the countries including West Germany and Sweden have already reached their targets.

However, partly as a result of further EEC pressure, the government started drafting a Green Bill in 1989, setting out plans to fit anti-pollution equipment to coal power stations and reduce sulphur dioxide emissions by 60% before the year 2000, as well as cutting emissions of nitrogen oxide, which contributes to the greenhouse effect, by 30%. The total programme will cost about £2 billion and will lead to higher electricity bills.

# ACID RAIN

## Effects

**Forests.**    According to a 1987 survey of forest damage throughout Europe, compiled for the UN's Cooperative Programme for the Monitoring and Evaluation of Long Range Transmission of Air Pollutants in Europe, the UK has the highest percentage of damaged forests in Europe. 67% of our conifer forests have slight to severe damage, and 28.9% have moderate to severe damage.

**Crops.**    Ozone pollution can reduce the yield of sensitive horticultural crops such as peas, lettuce, spinach and radish in most summers in the South of England, according to a report by the Terrestrial Effects Review Group of the Department of the Environment, in September 1988.

**Rivers/lochs.**    Over 120 Welsh rivers and at least 57 Scottish lochs are acidified.
Source: Friends of the Earth 1989.

**Wales.**    After 100 years of coal-burning the lower Swansea Valley is nearly bare of vegetation.
Source: Andre Singer, Battle for the Planet 1987.

**Scandinavia.**    Winds blow nearly two-thirds of Britain's sulphur emissions away — mainly towards Scandinavia. Over 600,000 tonnes of sulphur are deposited in Sweden each year and only 100,000 tonnes are actually generated there. 20,000 of Sweden's 90,000 lakes are acidified to some degree. 80% of lakes and streams in the southern half of Norway are technically dead or in a critical condition.
Source: Andre Singer, Battle for the Planet 1987.

## Trends

Sulphur dioxide emissions are down from nearly 5 million tonnes in 1976. Most sulphur dioxide

**The New Forest**

(2,600,000 tonnes in 1986) is emitted by power stations.

SOURCES: Warren Spring Laboratory, Department of Trade and Industry; The Earth Report 1988; John Williams, article, '£2 billion to stop acid rain', Evening Standard, 25.4.88.

# TOXIC WASTE

**Landfill site in the West Midlands**

## 35% of licensed landfill sites are potential risks (England and Wales, 1989)

Both Britain's waste disposal methods and the public control of those methods have attracted a great deal of adverse publicity. A report by the Pollution Inspectorate has shown that **over 70% of waste dumps have no control measures to stop unplanned leaks of methane gas**, which comes from rotting waste and can cause explosions. The report also found that 756 high-risk dumps lie within 250 metres of housing and industry.

In addition, Britain is importing large quantities of hazardous waste, and in danger of becoming the dustbin of Europe.

Source: Hansard 28.11.88.

### Methods

Most waste is disposed of by landfill. That can mean, at the simplest, digging and filling a hole in the ground, or creating a 'containment' site with a special lining of impermeable material. But no material is ultimately impermeable, and in the USA the landfilling of hazardous wastes is to be phased out completely by 1990. It is still defended in the UK.

### Public controls

Britain is unique in Western Europe as its hazardous waste disposal is handled almost entirely by private enterprise in a system described as 'ramshackle and antediluvian' by Sir Richard Southwood, a former chairman of the Royal Commission on Environmental Protection.

- Anyone, regardless of qualifications, can get a licence to operate a waste disposal site, provided they have planning permission and do not risk public health or water pollution.
- Site operators are not liable to prosecution after they hand in their licence — the Pollution Inspectorate has called for the closing of this legal loophole.
- Site licences are often granted without making operators state where the most dangerous wastes are placed — this was true of 85% of sites examined in one 1986 government survey.
- Many sites do not know what waste they are handling and have no equipment to test for dangerous waste.
- Only 23 of England's 75 local authorities had by September 1988 produced plans for dealing with wastes (though they were required by law in 1978).
- The Controlled Waste Inspectorate which monitors local authorities had only five inspectors in 1987. David Mills, its Chief Inspector, resigned in mid-1987, when Ministers refused to increase his staff.

Source: Geoffrey Lean and Eileen MacDonald, Britain's Dirty Business, Observer, 4.9.1988.

SOURCE: First Annual Report, HM Inspectorate of Pollution HMSO, March 89.

# 'DIRTY MAN OF EUROPE'

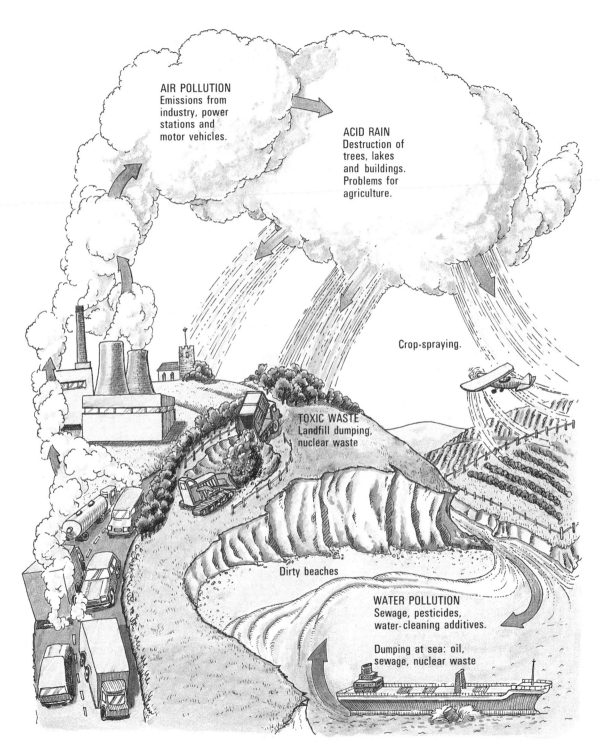

AIR POLLUTION
Emissions from industry, power stations and motor vehicles.

ACID RAIN
Destruction of trees, lakes and buildings. Problems for agriculture.

Crop-spraying.

TOXIC WASTE
Landfill dumping, nuclear waste

Dirty beaches

WATER POLLUTION
Sewage, pesticides, water-cleaning additives.

Dumping at sea: oil, sewage, nuclear waste

# NUCLEAR WASTE

**Sellafield**

## It will cost £4.3 billion to dispose of nuclear waste produced by the year 2000

Critics of nuclear power point out that it is not only more dangerous and expensive than coal-fired power stations, but also much more costly than originally promised, and can be more expensive than coal-fired power stations. The Central Electricity Generating Board now argues for nuclear power, more on the grounds of diversity than cost. The figures quoted here are merely for the cost of *disposing* of nuclear waste, which is so high that it may deter potential investors when the electricity industry is privatised in 1990, quite apart from the massive cost of decommissioning nuclear power stations.

There is an intense debate about how successfully nuclear waste can be disposed of and, even more, about how harmful are the effects of nuclear power stations. There can be no debate that the very existence of nuclear power involves great dangers — such as a repetition of Chernobyl, or the seizure of nuclear materials by terrorists.

# NUCLEAR WASTE

## Costs

**Disposal.** The total cost of £4.3 billion for disposing of nuclear waste by the year 2000 was put together by The Observer from three different estimates. The disposal costs of high-level nuclear waste will be £1.6 billion; of intermediate-level waste will be £1.08 billion; and of low-level waste will be £1.62 billion.

### Decommissioning power stations.
British Nuclear Fuels has estimated a total liability for decommissioning nuclear power stations of £4,605 million.
Source: Hansard 12.4.89.

## Effects

**Pollution.** The Irish Sea is said to be the most radioactive in the world, mainly because of the amount of low-level waste pumped out from the Cumbrian reprocessing plant of Sellafield. In 1984, Sellafield discharged about 2.2 million gallons of liquid radioactive waste a day into the Irish Sea.

**Health.** 19 children living within 20 miles of the Sellafield nuclear plant have developed leukaemia. Their parents are in the process of suing British Nuclear Fuels for compensation.
A variety of studies point to this excess of childhood leukaemia around nuclear installations. The Nation's Health, while reviewing and agreeing with the studies' findings, also points to other research which suggests that radiation levels around installations are too low to explain the increased leukaemia. (According to the National Radiological Protection Board, radioactive waste from nuclear power accounted for only *0.1%* of the total dose of radiation per head in 1987 in the UK.) The Nation's Health comments that radiation may have been underestimated, or repeated low-level radiation may be more dangerous than we think. More research is needed and, it concludes, the effects of nuclear power stations need to be compared with other sources of energy such as coal 'which has almost certainly been responsible for larger numbers of deaths and injuries than has nuclear power, both among those working in the industries and in the wider community'.
Sources: Marine Conservation Society; ed. Alwyn Smith and Bobbie Jacobson, The Nation's Health 1988.

## Imported nuclear waste
Britain is a major reprocessor of international nuclear waste. According to Michael Spicer, Under Secretary of State for Energy, the Thorp reprocessing plant at Sellafield, which has signed £2 billion of business with Japan, is the country's largest earner of yen.
Source: Hansard 12.4.89.

## Success?
The government gave permission in March 1989 for test drilling at Sellafield and Dounreay for a mine deep enough to hold most of the nuclear waste expected to be generated by 2050. But success is not assured. According to opponents, it is not yet proven that subterranean rock and engineered structures will stop radioactivity escaping.

SOURCES: The Observer, 20.11.88; report, Magnox Fuel Dry Storage and Direct Disposal, Assessment of CEGB/SSEB Reports (unpublished), Department of the Environment, December 1988; The Guardian 15.3.89.

# WATERWAY POLLUTION

**25,253
incidents reported (England
and Wales, 1987-88)
1,402 were 'serious
incidents' and only
288 led to prosecutions**

The pollution of British inland waterways and coastal waters has come in for increasing attention with the government's plans to privatise the water authorities. Agricultural waste is as much to blame as industrial waste. The two main forms of farm waste — slurry and silage effluent — can actually be much more toxic. 'Undiluted farm slurry is up to 100 times more polluting than untreated sewage. Silage liquor is even stronger at 200 times as powerful' according to the Water Authorities Association.

The consequences of pollution have often been disastrous. Fish life in many rivers has become extinct and more than a fifth of freshwater species are now under threat. Human beings have also suffered.

The government has not been very rigorous in prosecuting polluters, and green bodies such as Friends of the Earth are justifiably worried about the consequences of privatisation. On the other hand, the government argues that it is pursuing the most effective policy, and has promised that a National River Authority will police the 10 water authorities after privatisation.

Source: report, Water Pollution From Farm Waste 1988, Water Authorities Association.

## Who?

**Sewage works.** One in five sewage works run by the water authorities themselves regularly break pollution laws. These works, which daily treat 3.5 billion gallons of waste from homes, farms and factories, regularly discharge effluents into rivers that are so toxic they break the law.

**Companies.** Among the many companies breaching their permitted levels of discharge into British waters between August 1987 and July 1988 was the cream of British industry, including: British Petroleum, British Leyland, British Rail, British Creameries, the CEGB, British Gas, British Coal, British Tissues, Morphy-Richards and Rowntree Mackintosh.

**Prosecutions.** Many prosecuted companies have received fines of only a few hundred pounds or a conditional discharge. One Humberside chemical company whose spillage dyed the River Hull blue only received a conditional discharge.

## Effects

**Fishless rivers.** A combination of acid rain and industrial and agricultural waste has led to many of our rivers being completely fishless, including much of the River Mersey and its tributaries — now considered to be Europe's dirtiest river basin.

**Threatened species.** 12 out of Britain's 55 freshwater species of fish are endangered by pollution, including varieties of whitefish such as powan, schelly and vendace, and two members of the herring family — the allis shad and the twaite shad.

**Case history.** As a consequence of swimming into the polluted River Aire in North Yorkshire to save a man trying to drown himself, Police Inspector Malcolm Beavers became very

# WATERWAY POLLUTION

sick with post-viral fatigue syndrome. This condition can result from contact with water contaminated by bacteria from sewage works, and includes symptoms such as loss of physical strength, memory and concentration. After a year on sick leave, Beavers, a father of two, had to quit his job.

Source: Sunday Times 13.11.1988.

**King's Cross Canal**

## Costs

Nicholas Ridley told the commons in December, 1988 that it would cost £1 billion to bring sewage treatment works within the law. But that excludes the cost of repairing and replacing storm sewage overflows, which could cost another £637 million, according to Sir Hugh Rossi, chairman of the Commons environment committee.

## Regions

Water pollution is at its worst in the industrial centres of the Midlands and North, but southern rivers and lakes have also been affected. Anglian Water's sewage works had the worst record in England and Wales in 1987, with **one in three of its sewage works** operating illegally, although the chairman, Bernard Henderson, insisted that this was because they tested for pollution more often, rather than actually breaking the law more than anyone else.

## Trends

Total pollution incidents reported have nearly doubled since 1982-83 when there were 12,300.

SOURCES: Water Facts, Water Authorities Association; article, 'Water bosses', Sunday Times 12.3.89.

# DRINKING WATER

**Crop spraying in East Anglia**

## Widespread breaches of EC limits on pollutants

A variety of pollutants from a variety of sources are now entering our drinking water, including nitrates in fertilisers and pesticides from farms, aluminium from sewage works, and chlorinated solvents from industry. The quantities of these pollutants may not yet be dangerous, but if present trends continue, our tap water may become undrinkable.

## TOO MANY NITRATES AND PESTICIDES

**There were 298 breaches of EC limits on pesticides in drinking water between mid-1985 and mid-1987.**

In January 1989, the European Commission started legal proceedings against Britain for widespread breaches of EC limits on pesticides in drinking water, as a result of a report and subsequent complaint by Friends of the Earth listing 298 specific breaches. At the time of writing, in April 1989, it seems that the Government now has plans to tackle excessive nitrate levels, and will alter the Water Bill to give

156

# DRINKING WATER

legal force to EC standards — and intends to avoid Britain being hauled up in front of the European Court yet again.

In the worst areas of Britain — East Anglia especially — nitrate levels are twice the EC legal limit of 50 parts per million. Nitrates in fertilisers filter through underground reservoirs and contaminate drinking water. They can cause cancer and methaemoglobinaemia (blue baby syndrome) which deprives blood of oxygen and can kill. The problem is getting worse as farmers use more chemical fertilisers and pesticides to increase yields.

Sources: An Investigation of Pesticides in Drinking Water in England and Wales, Friends of the Earth, November 1988; Daily Mail 29.9.1988.

## TOO MUCH ALUMINIUM
**Over 3.5 million people in Britain drink water containing excess aluminium.**

People in over 50 areas of England and Wales drink water with levels of aluminium higher than the EC regulation of 200 micrograms of aluminium a litre (which may itself be too lax). Such water creates a 50 per cent greater risk of people contracting Alzheimer's disease. Aluminium is used in water treatment works to remove discoloration in peaty water. Among those affected are 1.15 million people in Birmingham, and over 900,000 in the Newcastle upon Tyne and Gateshead areas.

Source: Confidential minutes of Council of the Water Authorities Association meeting, 18.5.1988 — leaked to Friends of the Earth, reported in The Observer, 12.6.1988.

## TOO MANY CHLORINATED SOLVENTS

Underground water supplies which account for a third of Britain's drinking water are becoming increasingly polluted. Among the worst pollutants are cancer-causing chlorinated solvents such as trichloroethylene and tetrachloroethylene (used in the engineering and car industry in leather processing and dry cleaning).

One survey made for the government in 1985 by Imperial College and Leicester University showed that 61 out of 168 groundwater sources used for drinking supplies contained trichloroethylene. Five contained 50 micrograms per litre, when the World Health Organisation has laid down an interim level of 30. The highest level was 204 micrograms.

## The Camelford Incident
On 6 July 1988, 20 tonnes of alum were accidentally dumped into mains water at a treatment works on Bodmin Moor. The solution was 6,000 times the permitted EC maximum concentration per litre.

20,000 people in 7,000 households in the Camelford area were affected: bleached-blonde hair turned to green; tap water felt sticky and turned blue; bathing in or drinking the water led to diarrhoea, vomiting, blisters, sore throats and mouth ulcers. Five weeks later, many still suffered from lethargy, aches, pains and arthritis, and after seven weeks two-thirds of homes still received water with alum levels over EC limits.

# BEACHES

## 33%
## of bathing beaches polluted (GB, 1988)

(ie, had more than the maximum counts allowed by the EEC of 10,000 coliforms (intestine bacteria) per 100 ml of seawater.)

Britain was required by an EEC directive in 1979 to identify the sites 'where bathing is traditionally practised by large numbers of bathers,' and test the seawater for pollution. After initial reluctance — we only nominated 27, compared with more than 3,000 in France and Italy — Britain finally nominated 392 sites. Only 51% passed EEC standards in 1986. Of course, there are arguments about the stringency and validity of these standards, but they do serve as a rough guide, and it is generally agreed that too much sewage and industrial and farmland pollution continues to enter our seawater.

The water authorities are tackling the problem — and the government has earmarked about £600 million to clean up Britain's beaches altogether by 1995. There is still concern about whether that target will be met and, if it is, about the cost in increased water charges to the general public.

Source: Commons written answer, Michael Howard, Environment Minister, 22.2.1989.

## Source
Over 400 outfalls discharge sewage into Britain's coastal waters. 227 of them, serving a total of 1,700,000 people, discharge *untreated* sewage, even though this is now widely acknowledged as totally unacceptable.

## How much?
Over 300 million gallons of sewage are disposed of in our coastal waters every day. Most is untreated or only macerated (mashed up).

## Where?
Among the more notable contaminated bathing sites in 1985 were Scarborough, Southend and Weston-Super-Mare. Scarborough is visited by over 50,000 people in summer. Blackpool has also been identified by Greenpeace. 191 beaches in Britain are near an outfall discharging sewage and serving over 2,000 people.

Sources: Digest of Environmental Protection and Water Statistics 1986.

## Effects
Bathers in sewage-polluted waters can contract gastroenteritis, ear, nose and throat infections and skin irritations. Research in the USA shows 18 out of every 1,000 such bathers will become ill — here the corresponding figure is 31 out of every 1,000, (since our beaches are more polluted).

## International comparison
Britain has the most polluted bathing waters of any country conforming to European Community standards. Denmark with 76% "clean" waters, Italy (81%), France and Ireland (81%), and the Netherlands (93%) all put us to shame.

Source: EC Quality of Bathing Water report, 1986.

SOURCE: Marine Conservation Society.

**Blackpool beach**

# SEA POLLUTION

**Ocean incinerator at work**

The UK is acknowledged to be one of the worst polluters of the sea, dumping many things in the sea that we either shouldn't or have agreed not to. The pollution is in many instances hard if not impossible to measure, but we can certainly witness the after-effects — the dead seals, birds and other wildlife that wash up on our shores.

## WE STILL DUMP:

**Toxic waste.**    Britain still burns toxic waste at sea in the North Sea on incinerator ships, though this is forbidden in the Baltic, Mediterranean and America. Where highly toxic chemicals are involved, combustion efficiency has to be 99.99% if there is to be no environmental contamination, and the Marine Conservation Society suspects that efficiency is on average far below that required.

**Sewage sludge.**    Britain is the only European country still to dump sewage in the North Sea, although it agreed to stop in 1984. According to Britain's Water Authorities Association, agreeing to a ban on sewage dumping at sea would cost Britain over £100 million in new equipment and running costs.

Source: Earth Report, 1988.

**Pit waste.**    British Coal dumped millions of tons of pit waste (dust and sludge) in the North Sea in 1988 — 320,000 gallons every day — destroying several square miles of seabed off the Durham coast, turning the coastline black, killing sea-life and putting fishermen out of business. The Northumbria water authority has told British Coal that dumping can continue for another four years.

Source: article, John Rowland, 'Pit waste turns North Sea black', Sunday Times, December 1988.

SOURCE: Marine Conservation Society.

# 139
# reported oil spills (GB, 1985)

## Where?

The oil spills came all round Great Britain. The incidents included: 30 in East Scotland; 22 in Essex and Kent (including the Thames Estuary), 19 in Orkney and the Shetlands; and 17 in the Irish Sea.

## Cost

The total cost to the authorities of cleaning up all the oil spilled in 1985 was £107,000.

## Worst incidents

The worst incidents in 1985 were:

- the loss of 400 tonnes of paraffin following a tank failure at the British Petroleum Terminal in 1985. Only 100 tonnes were later recovered.
- the escape of 300 tonnes of oily water into the Firth of Forth from a fractured pipeline at HM Dockyard at Rosyth.

## Trends

The number of oil spills fluctuates considerably. In 1981 there were 171, in 1983 there were 117.

SOURCE: Digest of Environmental Protection and Water Statistics 1986.

**Seabird victim of oil pollution**

# LOST HABITATS

As many natural habitats have been lost in the last 40 years as in the previous 400 years. The Royal Society for the Protection of Birds claims that the challenge to protect the countryside in the next 10 years is as great as that faced in the last 100 years.

Sources: Council for the Protection of Rural England, Royal Society for the Protection of Birds.

## 95% of hay meadows have been lost through agricultural intensification.

## 80% of chalk grasslands have been lost through conversion to arable or improved grassland.

## 40% of natural woodlands have been lost, in part by conversion to conifer plantation.

## 50% of marshes have been lost, mainly through drainage and reclamation operations.

## 65% of natural coastline has been lost.

## 22% of hedgerows have been lost, largely to farm cultivation.

Sources: Nature Conservation in Great Britain, Nature Conservancy Council 1984; Royal Society for the Protection of Birds.

## Extinct and endangered species

**Butterflies and dragonflies** have shown the biggest losses among flora and fauna. Their habitats have been most affected by agricultural intensification. The large blue butterfly became extinct in 1979 and four out of 43 species of dragonflies have become extinct since 1953.

**Reptiles and amphibians.** Four of our 12 species are endangered, including the sand lizard and natterjack toad.

**The otter** has become rare or disappeared in many parts of England and Wales.

**Bats.** Several of our 15 species of bats, particularly horseshoe and mouse-eared bats, are seriously endangered.

**Plants.** 10 species have been lost since 1930, and 117 species have declined 33% since 1930 — those endangered include the Early Spider Orchid, the Early Star of Bethlehem, Stinking Goosefoot and Martin's Ramping Fumitory.

**Birds.** Endangered or vulnerable species include:
*Woodlarks* — down to 210-30 pairs in 1983, mainly through habitat loss, especially lowland heaths; *Corncrakes* — down to about 450 calling males in Britain, mainly through habitat loss, especially hay meadows; *Roseate Terns* — down

# LOST HABITATS

to about 110 pairs in Britain; *Red Grouse* — vulnerable through poor moorland management; *Golden Eagles* — vulnerable with about 424 pairs in 1982; *Merlins* — our rarest falcon, vulnerable through loss of heather moorland, down to about 6,000-7,000 pairs; and the *Grey partridge* — has declined by some 80% in the last 30 years due to pesticides and herbicides removing food plants and invertebrates on which it depends.

SOURCES: Royal Society for the Protection of Birds; Nature Conservancy Council.

**Otter**

**Bat**

**Golden eagle**

**Red squirrel**

# COUNTRYSIDE

## Lost to urban sprawl (1947-80):
## 4,230 square kilometres of land (2.8% of total land mass of England and Wales)

The ever growing demand for new houses in the green belt and on greenfield sites has already swallowed up large areas of natural land, particularly grassland, and threatens to capture still more.

But environmentalists are if anything more concerned about what's happening on farmland, which the RSPB describes as 'in turmoil'. As farming has become ever more intensive over the last 40 years, great areas of grassland and woodland have been given over to cultivation, and considerable areas of moorland in turn have been given over to grassland. All this, together with the steady elimination of hedgerows, has resulted in the loss of many natural habitats and the extinction of many species of plants and wildlife, and leaves many other species still endangered.

## Privatisation
The Council for the Protection of Rural England is particularly concerned that when the water industry is privatised nearly half a million acres of countryside will be sold with it, including some of our most beautiful areas such as 15% of the Peak National Park, and we could see a wave of development.

## Land use
Roughly 80% of the UK is farmed land, 10% is woodland and forestry, and 10% is taken up by industry, roads and housing.

## Trends
The total proportion of farmed land has remained roughly constant over the years, but within that, cultivated land has increased from 28.1% of the total area of England and Wales to 35.4% between 1947-80. Hedgerow loss has increased from an average of 4,200 km a year between 1947-69 to 6,400 km for 1980-85.

SOURCES: Monitoring Landscape Change, Department of the Environment 1986; Royal Society for the Protection of Birds.

# DERELICT AND VACANT LAND

**Derelict land in east London**

## 133,000 acres of land in England and Wales are derelict
## 494,000 acres of land are vacant

There are large areas of land in Britain — up to 40% of the green belt in England and Wales — which are derelict, i.e. 'incapable of beneficial use without treatment', but also capable of being reclaimed. Examples are the sites of old quarries and open-cast mines, and former hospitals, which can be found in or around most cities, from London and Swansea to Leeds and Glasgow. There are also large areas of vacant land — buildings lying empty, open land, fields, even rubbish tips — which are unused. The total of 518,000 acres of vacant land is equivalent to the whole of Nottinghamshire. Much of this wasteland is concentrated in inner cities — as much as 10% of inner Liverpool and Glasgow.

When the demand for new space for housing and industry is so strong, it is vital that we use all existing resources before cutting into new green belt. The Countryside Commission, the government's advisory body on rural affairs in England and Wales, is starting to tackle the problem of derelict land. It should have planted two urban forests on derelict land in the summer of 1989, probably in the Black Country and Tyneside, and has plans for many more. The Scottish Office also has plans for Glasgow and Edinburgh. The idea is to create settings for such things as theme parks, science parks, motorcycle trail parks and even art galleries.

## Unused land in public ownership

At the end of March 1989, there were 84,200 acres of unused or underused land in 'public ownership', including land owned by local authorities and nationalised industries. Over 31,000 of these acres were in inner city areas, such as Hackney or Birmingham, covered by the government's urban programme and therefore eligible for grants.

## Trends

Derelict land in England alone has decreased by 9% from almost 113,000 acres in 1982 to 102,500 acres in 1988. Vacant land was reduced by 4,200 acres in 1988 and by 3,600 a year in each of the previous three years.

Sources: Department of Environment; Welsh Office; Michael Chisholm and Philip Kivell, Inner City Waste Land, Institute of Economic Affairs 1987.

# MONUMENTS AND BUILDINGS

**Stonehenge**

## 2% of England's known archaeological resource has protected monument status

Statutory protection has only been extended so far to 13,000 ancient monuments and sites — about 2% of England's archaeological resource. At the same time a Monuments Protection Programme will be in full operation in 1989 and scheduling is being speeded up. The threat to ancient sites is not so much from development pressures as from agricultural practices, vandalism and neglect. It was estimated a while ago that as many as 200 nationally important monuments are lost each year.

## There are 413,000 listed buildings in England

Our historic buildings are much better protected than those of other countries. In Ireland, for example, according to Desmond Fitzgerald, there are only about 30 surviving major country houses, and hundreds have disappeared this century, either destroyed or demolished. About 60% of local authorities now have full-time conservation or archaeology officers.

Source: Observer, 12.2.1989.

## Trends

The number of listed buildings is up from 313,500 in 1984, and 800 new conservation areas have been added.

SOURCE: English Heritage.

## Litter: 'a dirty nation'

'Our streets, our roads and motorways, our railways lines and stations, the outskirts of our towns are often filthy. Old bedsteads in ditches; rubble tipped behind hedges; scrap cars abandoned in thickets — we have all seen it. . . . The problem is so severe that local people need stronger weapons than dust-pan and brush to get something done about it. . . .'

Nicholas Ridley, Minister for the Environment, declared in March 1989 that Britain was a 'dirty nation' and announced plans for new laws to force local councils to clean up the streets and empower people to call their local authorities to account if they failed to do so.

Source: Nicholas Ridley, speech to Conservative central council, Scarborough, 18.3.1989.

# TRAFFIC JAMS

## The average speed of traffic in central London in 1986-88 was 11 miles per hour

If urban civilisation hasn't quite ground to a halt, that's how it sometimes feels in the capital's traffic jams. Quite apart from the inconvenience to the ordinary driver, **London's dilapidated and inadequate transport system costs business about £15 billion a year and threatens Britain's economic renaissance**, according to a recent CBI report. Emergency services are also affected. Ambulances which reached accidents at an average 25 mph in 1975 now barely average 11 mph.

The answers to London's traffic problems seem to lie more in traffic management schemes (such as car pools) and in charging road-users, than in building extra roads. The CBI report recommended a whole range of measures including cracking down on parking, flexible four-day working weeks, a Docklands light rail or Tube line extended into Kent, more crossings over the Thames, and converting underutilised rail lines to roads.

### When?
Average traffic speeds, 1986-88, were 11 mph for the evening peak and daytime off-peak periods, and 11.5 mph for the morning peak period.

### Costs
In the CBI report, among individual company estimates of losses due to congestion each year were: British Gas — £2 million; Royal Mail Letters — £10.4 million; Marks and Spencer — £2 million, and British Telecom — £7.25 million.

The cost just to users of the Earl's Court one-way system is estimated at around £11 million a year by the Department of Transport.

### Trends
Apart from the occasional burst of speed, average traffic speeds have fallen gradually from 14.2 mph (morning peak) and 13.2 mph (evening peak) in 1974-76.

SOURCES: Department of Transport; The Capital At Risk, CBI, 29.3.89.

# ANIMAL EXPERIMENTS

## 3,112,051 animal experiments were carried out in Britain in 1986

The British Union for the Abolition of Vivisection points out that animals 'continue to be burnt, blinded, poisoned and driven insane in British laboratories'. Others point to the value of experiments in reducing human suffering and saving lives. BUAV will counter that experiments on animals do not always produce conclusive results about the effects on humans. It quotes Opren and Erladin as recent examples of animal-tested drugs withdrawn after serious and in some cases fatal side effects on people.

But, to judge by the falling numbers of experiments, some are unnecessary by any criteria, and, as recent publicity in the newspapers has shown, many experiments are unnecessarily cruel. Anti-vivisectionists insist that there are a variety of alternatives to live animals for experiments, including chemical analysis and molecular modelling of new drugs (which the National Anti-Vivisection Society estimates could save 400,000 laboratory animals in the UK alone), use of isolated organs and cells, and substitution of models, videos and computer programs for vivisection in education.

## Which animals?
1,622,138 experiments were conducted on mice, and 830,159 on rats, together accounting for 80% of total experiments. Guinea-pigs, rabbits, birds and fish were the other main animals, each of which was involved in between about 130,000 and 150,000 experiments.

## Without anaesthetics
The number of experiments carried out without anaesthesia was 2,275,400. Anaesthetics were used throughout the entire experiment in just 252,889 cases.

## Purpose of experiments
The purpose of about half the experiments (1,586,000) was 'to select, develop or study the use, etc. of medical, dental and veterinary products and appliances'. The purpose of 704,000 experiments was the 'study of normal or abnormal body structure or function'. 18% of experiments were performed to comply with the provisions of one Act or other, such as the Food and Drugs Act, or Medicines Act.

Cosmetics and toiletries according to official figures are involved in less than 0.5% of experiments — which still means 15,000 animals.

## Experimenters
There were 11,419 licensed experimenters in 1986, the majority of whom were universities (6,427) and commercial concerns (2,654). Others included polytechnics, quangos, government departments and public health labs.

## Trends
Animal experiments have been steadily falling — down from 5,385,000 in 1977. The 1986 figures are the lowest since 1957. But, the BUAV points out that, even assuming the recent rate of decline continues, 1,500,000 animals will still die in British laboratories in the year 2000.

SOURCE: Statistics of Experiments on Living Animals, Great Britain 1986.

# ANIMAL EXPERIMENTS

**Animal Rights**

The major goals of the animal rights movement are:

- the abolition of the use of animals in science;
- the end of commercial animal agriculture;
- the end of commercial and sport hunting and trapping;
- the end of zoos.

The moral basis of these goals is the belief that animals have intrinsic if not equal rights and inherent value. The human race is guilty of 'speciesism' comparable to racism. Not all animal liberationists share the above goals. Some are only against factory farmings, others support important medical experiments, such as for cancer research.

# ANIMALS DESTROYED

## When the Government killed the dog licence they left us to kill the dogs.

One thousand dogs are killed in Britain every day.

For the most part, healthy dogs and puppies with years of life left in them.

The killings take place at local vets, in RSPCA centres and other animal charities throughout the country.

The dogs are given an over-dose of anaesthetic and die within seconds.

A van makes regular collections and the dead dogs are taken to the local incinerator.

It doesn't take long to turn a Jock, Spot or Sandy into a small pile of ashes.

This daily slaughter is strange work for a society founded to prevent cruelty to animals.

We hate the killing.

We are sick of doing the Government's dirty work behind closed doors.

We want you to help us force through a dog registration scheme.

The dogs we kill are home-less. Unwanted, or strays left

to roam the streets and parks, often in packs.

There are at least 500,000 of them out there right now.

Left to themselves, the figure would be close to 4 million in ten years' time.

Homeless dogs cause road ac-cidents, attack livestock and foul our parks and pavements.

And yet we can't blame the dogs, for we live in a society that makes it more difficult to own a television than a living, breathing creature.

There is no licence required. The Government abolished the licence last year and we are now seeing the consequences.

The RSPCA want to see a dog registration scheme intro-duced.

And so it seems do most of you. In a recent poll, 92% of you said "yes" to registration.

If there was a registration fee it would encourage responsible dog-ownership.

Each dog could be identified with a number so that its owner

could be traced and held respon-sible for the dog's actions.

The money raised would finance a national dog warden scheme, more efficient clean-up operations and more education for dog-owners.

These measures seem so sensible you wonder why they haven't been tried before.

Well, many of them have.

Sweden, America, Germany, Australia, Russia, France and Ireland all have a more enlight-ened policy than Britain.

Help us catch up.

Write to your MP and press for dog registration.

If you're not sure how to go about it, call free on 0800 400478 and we'll give you an action-pack and add your name to our petition.

Do it now, for every day that goes by sees another 1,000 dogs put down.

And what kind of society kills healthy dogs? (RSPCA)

Registration, not extermination.

**RSPCA campaign poster**

## Over 365,000 healthy but unwanted stray dogs are destroyed every year

## 134,150 animals humanely destroyed by the RSPCA in 1987

For a supposedly animal-loving nation we kill an awful lot of animals. The figure of total dogs killed throughout the country is an estimate, but that of animals destroyed by the RSPCA in 1987 is

precise, and includes 61,615 dogs and 52,343 cats. All these animals are destroyed at places like dogs' homes, police kennels, and the surgeries of vets. Some of them are unwanted gifts at Christmas, many are pets returned by their owner. A spokesman at Battersea Dogs' Home expressed amazement at how many people bring in a dog on a lead saying, 'I just found it.'

The RSPCA has complained that the responsibility for killing has been unfairly foisted on it by the government and argues that much of the killing could be avoided if the government were to operate a registration scheme of dogs and owners.

# ANIMALS SLAUGHTERED

**Abattoir in Derbyshire**

**526,000,000 chickens, 31,900,000 turkeys/geese 15,807,000 pigs, 15,673,000 sheep, 8,100,000 ducks and 4,113,000 cattle were slaughtered in Britain in 1987**

Our hunger for white meat grows ever more voracious. Since 1981 when 412.4 million chickens were slaughtered, we have killed more chickens every year — and more turkeys and geese, and more ducks (except for a slight dip in 1987).

We keep our animals in often appalling conditions. According to Sir Richard Body, MP and former chairman of the Commons select committee on agriculture:

- 10,000 chickens or turkeys may be kept in a single building from soon after they're hatched till slaughter;

- most breeding sows are penned in stalls with room only to stand up or lie down in, but not to move around;

- pigs can be kept in total darkness to discourage the fighting that comes about through boredom.

Hardly surprising then that 1988 should have seen significant and much publicised outbreaks of salmonella in eggs and listeria in chilled foods.

SOURCE: Ministry of Agriculture.

'A recent report told of a live broiler chicken found by the roadside, presumably having fallen from a lorry on its way to slaughter. The bird was literally being eaten alive by maggots. The vet who saw the bird was shocked, commenting that there may be many chickens in such a condition inside broiler houses during hot summer weather.'

Source: Janet Hunt, The Holistic Cook 1986.

# ANIMAL HUNTING

## 12,000
## foxes are killed in hunts every year

### Fox hunting

Fox hunts kill between 12,000 and 13,000 foxes a year according to a survey by Dr Stephen Harris of Bristol University in 1987. He points out that this does not help control the fox population, since the figures represent only 2.5% of the fox population, which can survive an annual mortality rate of up to 70% and still recover. So 12,000 foxes die annually for sport.

### Hare hunting

New Scientist was already worried in the early 1980s that 'hares are steadily disappearing from the British countryside'. So was Game Conservancy magazine which found good evidence of a gradual decline, both 'substantial and serious', in the brown hare ever since the 1960s.

Sources: New Scientist, 10.3.83, Game Conservancy, 11.3.82.

### Stag hunting

Deer are hunted by three packs of hounds in the West Country — the Tiverton, Quantock and Devon and Somerset Staghounds — and by one pack of hounds in the New Forest, the New Forest Buckhounds.

### Mink hunting

This has replaced the bloodsport of otter hunting, and now alternates with the fox hunting season between August and April.

SOURCE: League against Cruel Sports.

**Lynx anti-fur campaign poster**

# CHARITIES

## Contributions: £103 (average per household, GB, 1987) — 1% of average disposable household income

While statistics on donations to charities are very unreliable as they depend heavily on interviewees' memories, the above figures give a rough idea of total British charitability. Is 1% of our income enough?

Only 46% of interviewees in the Charities Aid Foundation survey agreed that they have a responsibility to give what they can to charity. Britons have traditionally looked to the Welfare State to provide many welfare functions. Pollsters have shown time and time again that the majority of us agree that more money should be spent on hospitals, schools, and helping the poor — although we are less willing to pay the extra taxes needed.

One practical difficulty faced by charities is a general suspicion towards them — nearly half of interviewees in the above survey thought little of the money given to the bigger charities reaches the cause.

### Who?

The pattern of donation is very skewed — almost 40% of households gave only £1 or less per month to charity. Only 5% gave more than £30 per month. People who see themselves as better off and people for whom religion is important tend to give more.

**M/F.** More men (53%) than women (38%) interviewed by the CAF survey had done no volunteering in the past 3 months.

**Companies.** Charitable cash donations by business and industry total £135 million a year.

Source: 'A Guide to Company Giving', The Directory of Social Change, 1989.

## How many charities?

According to the Charity Commission, there are about **160,000** charities.

## Charities' costs

One in five charities diverts more than 60% of funds towards administration, according to Robin Guthrie, the new chairman of the Charity Commission. He actually sees all the new charity income as coming from companies, the very rich and the relatively poor — not the prosperous, but tight, middle class — and fears this won't change until the favourite excises about waste and fraud are eliminated.

Source: article, Charity begins . . ., Sunday Times, 20.11.1988.

## Top 10 charities

(by voluntary income, excluding rents, investments, grants, fees, etc., 1986 figures)

| | | |
|---|---|---|
| 1. | Oxfam | £42.7 m |
| 2. | Save the Children | £32.8 m |
| 3. | R.B. Lifeboat Institution | £28.8 m |
| 4. | National Trust | £28.3 m |
| 5. | Imperial Cancer Research Fund | £27.3 m |
| 6. | Cancer Research Campaign | £22.6 m |
| 7. | Dr Barnardo's | £22.2 m |
| 8. | Salvation Army | £20.4 m |
| 9. | Band Aid Trust | £15 m |
| 10. | Guide Dogs for the Blind Association | £13.7 m |

## International comparison

American individuals donated an estimated 2.05% of personal income in 1987 — around $77 billion.

## Trends

The average household contribution recorded by the 1985-86 Charity Household Survey was only £70. But the rise may be mainly due to inflation and better recording techniques. It does seem, though, that people give more as their income rises.

## Charities' total income: £12.7 billion (UK, 1985)

Voluntary donations account for a relatively small percentage of charities' total income. Most comes from fees and charges for the services they offer, such as homes for the elderly and schools for the handicapped, and from rents on their properties and investments. The above total was for 1985 and may well be around £15 billion by now.

| Fund raising (including by individuals and companies) | £1.9 bn |
|---|---|
| Fees and charges | £7.7 bn |
| Rents and investments | £1.4 bn |
| Granst from statutory bodies | £1.4 bn |
| Commercial activities etc. | £0.3 bn |
| Total | £12.7 bn |

Source: John Posnet, Trends in the Income of Registered Charities, 1980-5; Charity Trends.

SOURCE: 1987 Charity Household Survey, Charities Trends, 11th Edition.

# WHAT IS THE COST OF ABOLISHING POVERTY?

Alan Walker

Professor of Social Policy, University of Sheffield

Poverty is one of the most persistent social problems described in this book. A solution to poverty is urgently required because, rather than diminishing as Britain becomes a more and more affluent society, it is growing rapidly (by 55 per cent between 1979 and the last year for which official figures are available, 1985) and there is a danger that the widening divide between rich and poor will result in permanent and embittering social fractures. Also there is a close causal link between poverty and other forms of social deprivation, for example in education, housing and health, many of which would disappear if those concerned had adequate incomes to live on.

The purpose of this short essay is to review the cost of attempting to tackle this most fundamental of all social problems and, thereby, undermining many of the other problems outlined by Michael Tintner in *State Imperfect*.

## Defining poverty

Most people agree that poverty should be defined in relative rather than absolute terms. In other words, poverty is regarded as the level of income below which people lack the means required to participate in the ordinary life of the community in which they live, rather than the point at which they reach destitution or near-starvation. This does not mean that the definition of poverty is uncontroversial, a fact emphasised by the recent speech by the former Secretary of State for Social Security, John Moore. He argued that 'it is utterly absurd to speak as if one in three people today is in dire need' (Moore, 1989, p. 1). Although Mr Moore had to recognise subsequently that this claim had never been made by the poverty lobby, he succeeded in reopening the dispute between those who define poverty in absolute and those who define it in relative terms. Mr Moore associated himself firmly with the absolutists by arguing that in terms of nineteenth century poverty low-income families today have 'affluence beyond their wildest dreams'. Of course, if poverty is defined according to the Dickensian standards of a hundred years ago then very few people in modern Britain face the same squalor and privation. **Thus, by definition, poverty may be abolished by the stroke of a pen or the turn of a phrase.**

However, in case anyone is tempted to accept this convenient 'solution', its full implications must be understood. In the first place it means that the poverty line is not linked to current living standards but instead is fixed historically. Some idea of what this implies for those who would otherwise be defined as poor can be grasped by imagining the impact of applying a similar reference point to wages and salaries.

Most employees would, with good reason, be outraged at the suggestion that their living standards should be measured against Victorian ones. Secondly, therefore, the absolute approach tends towards a condescending view of the poor by proposing for them a style of life that is significantly different than that enjoyed by the rest of society. Thirdly, it ignores the fact the lifestyles and consumption, including diet, are determined more by social convention than scientific judgment and, as a result, they change over time.

For these reasons most experts have adopted a relative concept. There are various different methods used to measure poverty relative to current living standards but the most commonly used, and the one adopted in this book, is the minimum Social Security benefit rates operating in any country. In Britain these are the Income Support (formerly Supplementary Benefit) levels paid to families of different composition. This approach has the advantage that these benefit levels are reviewed and uprated annually by Parliament and, therefore, may be regarded as officially approved minimum income standards. On the other hand, since they are now increased only in line with inflation, when earnings exceed inflation, as they have done over the last decade, the living standards of the poor lag behind those of average wage and salary earners, and the usefulness of Income Support as a relative measure of poverty begins to be called into question.

# Abolishing poverty

Using a relative standard means that we cannot simply abolish poverty by reference to a 100-year-old poverty line. Nor is it simply a matter of increasing economic growth and hoping that the fruits of this entrepreneurial activity will 'trickle down' to the poor. As the many volumes of evidence of the last 10 years show, the poor have actually got poorer while the rich have got considerably richer (see p. 32, and Walker and Walker, 1987). Any serious attempt to abolish or singificantly relieve poverty implies two prerequisites: concerted action by central government, and a redistribution from the better-off to the poor. What form might such a redistribution take?

## Problem
The latest official Department of Social Security statistics (see p. 31) reveal that 9.4 million people were living on or below the state poverty line in 1985 and a further 6 million were hovering on the margins of poverty. **These would be the target groups and the aim of an anti-poverty strategy would be to raise their incomes to a specified level.** But what level?

## Solution
Scientific research (Townsend, 1979; Desai, 1986) suggests that there is a poverty 'threshold' **at around 150 per cent of the Income Support** levels, below which people's ability to participate in customary roles, relationships and consumptions becomes severely constrained. For the purpose of illustrating the likely cost of abolishing poverty, let us accept this threshold as our target income level. For a married couple with two children aged 11-15 with a current Income Support entitlement of £96, that represents £144 per week exclusive of housing costs, which compares with average national male earnings of £254 per week. For a lone parent aged 18 or over with one child aged under 11, currently entitled to £57.05 a week, it would be £85.57.

## Assumptions
The equivalent rates were calculated for pensioners, couples with and without children and people with disabilities. It was not possible to be precise about the ages of the children living in poverty and so these were estimated. For similar reasons the disabled child and severe disabilty premiums were also estimated.

   For families living on Income Support currently, a straightforward increase in their benefit rates of 50 per cent has been calculated. For those living below the poverty line an average deficit of 20 per cent has been assumed and, therefore, their incomes would be increased by 70 per cent.

Finally, for those living on the margins of poverty, an average excess of 20 per cent has been assumed and thus their incomes would be enhanced by 30 per cent to reach the 150 per cent of Income Support target. Again it must be emphasised that these are crude estimates for the purpose of illustration only.

## Cost

The cost of raising incomes of poor families to 150 per cent of Income Support levels would be, for:

|  | £ million |
|---|---|
| Families living on the poverty line | 6,400 |
| Families living below the poverty line | 3,325 |
| Families on the margins of poverty | 4,910 |
| Total: | £14,635 |

This is the cost of a **targeted** abolition of poverty, based on raising incomes of poor families to 150% of Income Support levels. It depends on people asking for means-tested benefits and would not therefore on its own be sufficient to abolish poverty. All means-tested benefits suffer from problems of stigma and low take-up — hence the numbers living *below* the poverty line.

In order to ensure that the increases reached all of those in need, a **universal** approach would be necessary, using benefits *paid as of right*, such as pensions, a national minimum wage and child benefits. A universal approach would be much more expensive, because here benefits also go to those who do not necessarily need them. (However, if the tax system was reformed to make it more progressive, much of this excess cost could be recouped.)

In addition, some poor people, notaby the disabled, require **additional** income to compensate for extra costs and disadvantages. The Disability Alliance (1987) put the total cost of a comprehensive disability income designed to abolish poverty among the disabled at £3,000 million.

**A universal approach to abolishing poverty through a combined benefit, tax and wages policy would cost, at a rough estimate, £25,000 million a year.**

How might such a sum be raised? The first point to make is that, over the last 10 years there has been a considerably greater redistribution towards the better-off. Thus, since 1979, the top 10 per cent of tax payers have received a cumulative total of just over £50,000 million in tax cuts compared with just under £1,000 million in cuts going to the bottom tenth. Moreover, **the sum required is less than half the current Social Security budget and only 0.007 per cent of Gross Domestic Product — or 15 per cent of total public expenditure**.

This modest sum, in national income terms, could easily be raised by a package of tax and national insurance contribution (NIC) changes, including an increase in the top rate of 70 per cent, a more progressive tax and NIC structure, restricting mortgage interest and pension relief to the basic rate of tax, and taxing pension fund income.

# Relieving poverty

If the goal of abolishing poverty was regarded as too ambitious, it is possible to do a great deal to relieve it at very little net cost to the Exchequer (Hills, 1989). A package of a net cost of just £600 million to the Exchequer could, for example, achieve the following:

- improve pensions and national insurance benefits by nearly one-fifth;
- double child benefit and one-parent benefit;
- increase Income Support rates by one-tenth; and
- restore recent cuts in housing benefits.

The gross cost of these changes and the consequent changes in other benefits would be **£11,600 million**. Virtually the whole of this sum could be raised through the reform of the tax and NIC structure. This would include the introduction of progressive NICs with no upper limit as at present, the abolition of personal tax allowances and their replacement by a zero rate band of £2,605 a year for each person, a graduated tax rate with a maximum of 50 per cent, and an investment income surcharge.

The impact of this package would be an average gain of around £8.50 per week for those in the bottom half of the income distribution, while the cost of the reform would come predominantly from the top 10 per cent of income recipients. Overall the net cost would be only £600 million, the exact amount the government is going to spend on the introduction of the independent taxation of husband and wife in 1990 (for full details see Hills, 1989).

Thus it is possible to relieve poverty considerably and, at the same time, lay the foundations of a progressive tax structure that could do considerably more, at negligible cost to the Treasury. It is also feasible to go much further and abolish poverty altogether, or at least on a significant scale. Whether we choose to do so rests on political priorities rather than the availability of resources. Britain is a rich nation, and as shown, the resources are not lacking. What is absent for the moment is the political will to tackle poverty and other social problems.

# References

M. Desai (1986) 'Drawing the Line: On Defining the Poverty Threshold' in P. Golding (ed.) *Excluding the Poor*, London, Child Poverty Action Group, pp. 1-20.

Disability Alliance (1987) *Poverty and Disability*, London, Disability Alliance.

J. Hills (1989) *Changing Tax*, London, Child Poverty Action Group.

J. Moore (1989) 'The End of the Line for Poverty', speech to the Greater London Area CPC, 11 May.

P. Townsend (1979) *Poverty in the United Kingdom*, Harmondsworth, Penguin Books.

A. Walker and C. Walker (eds) (1987) *The Growing Divide: A Social Audit 1979-1987*, London, Child Poverty Action Group.

# SOURCES AND REFERENCES

Adult Literacy Basic Skills Unit, *Literacy, Numeracy and Adults*, London, 1987.

Amnesty, *When The State Kills*, London, 1988.

*Annual Abstract of Statistics*, London, HMSO, annual.

H. Ashton, 'Dangers and Medico-legal Aspects of Benzodiazepines', *Journal of Medical Defence Union*, Summer 1987.

Association of Metropolitan Authorities, *Housing Facts*, 1988.

John Balding, *Young People in 1987*, Exeter University, 1988.

Patrick Barwise and Andrew Ehrenberg, *Television and its Audience*, London, 1989.

Benn, Coote and Gill, *The Rape Controversy*, London, NCCL, 1986.

Richard Berthoud, *The Reform of Supplementary Benefit*, Policy Studies Institute, 1984.

Richard Berthoud, *Credit, Debt and Poverty*, London, HMSO, 1989.

M. Blaxter, 'A Comparison of Measures of Inequality in Morbidity', in A.J. Fox (ed.), *Inequalities in Health within Europe*, Aldershot, 1988.

L. Burghes, *Children in Poverty*, Concern: National Children's Bureau, 50, 1984.

N. Butler, et al., *Handicapped Children: Their Homes and Lifestyles*, University of Bristol, 1978.

CBI, *The Capital At Risk*, 1989.

Charities Aid Foundation, *Charity Trends*, annual.

Child Poverty Action Group, *Poverty: The Facts*, London, 1988.

National Children's Home, *Children in Danger*, London, 1989.

Michael Chisholm and Philip Kivell, *Inner City Waste Land*, London, Institute of Economic Affairs, 1987.

*Cigarette Smoking: 1972 to 1986*, OPCS Monitor SS 1988.

Bronwen Cohen, *Caring for Children*, Commission of the European Communities, 1988.

B. Cox et al., *Health and Lifestyle Survey*, Health Promotion Research Trust, 1987.

Crime Prevention Unit, *Costs of Crime*, 1988.

*Criminal Statistics, England and Wales*, London, HMSO, annual.

Department of Education, *Statistical Bulletin*, 1985.

Department of the Environment, *English House Condition Survey, 1986*, London, 1988.

Department of the Environment, *Monitoring Landscape Change*, 1986.

Department of Transport, *Road Transport Statistics, 1986*.

Department of Transport, *Transport Statistics, 1976-86*.

Department of Health and Social Security, *Households Below Average Income, 1981-85*, 1988.

Department of Health and Social Security, *Low Income Families Statistics 1985*, 1988.

Department of Health and Social Security, *On the State of the Public Health*, 1987.

*Digest of Environmental Protection and Water Statistics*, HMSO, annual.

*Employment Gazette*, HMSO, monthly.

Equal Opportunities Commission, *Women and Men in Great Britain*, HMSO, 1987.

Angela Evans and Sue Duncan, *Responding to Homelessness: Local Authority Policy and Practice*, Department of the Environment, 1988.

*Family Expenditure Survey*, HMSO, annual.

*Fire Statistics*, HMSO, annual.

Friends of the Earth, *An Investigation of Pesticides in Drinking Water in England and Wales*, 1988.

*General Household Survey*, HMSO, annual.

# SOURCES AND REFERENCES

Edward Goldsmith and Nicholas Hildyard, *Earth Report*, London, 1988.

Paul Gordon and Anne Newnham, *Different Worlds*, Runnymede Trust, 1986.

H. Graham, *Caring for the Family*, Health Education Council, 1986.

Phil Greasley, *Men At Work*, LAGER (Lesbian and Gay Employment Rights), 1986.

*Great Britain*, HMSO, annual.

H. Green, *Informal Carers*, OPCS, (General Household Survey 1985 — GHS No. 15 Supplement A) HMSO.

Valerie Hammond, *Women in Management in Great Britain*, Ashridge Management College, 1988.

Brian Hayes, *Public Disorder Outside Metropolitan Areas*, Association of Chief Police Officers report, 1988.

*Health and Personal Social Services for England*, HMSO, annual.

A. Herxheimer, 'Some Problems with Benzodiazepines', *Drug & Therapeutics Bulletin*, Vol. 23, 21-23, 1985.

*Home Accident Surveillance System Report*, (now changed to *Home and Leisure Accident Research Report*), Department of Trade and Industry, annual.

Home Office, *Domestic Violence: An Overview of the Literature*, HMSO, 1989.

Home Office, *Report on the Work of the Prison Service*, 1987-88, HMSO.

Home Office, Research Study No. 85, *British Crime Survey*, 1984.

Home Office Statistical Bulletin, *Criminal Careers of those Born in 1953, 1958 and 1963*, Issue 7, 1985.

*Index on Censorship*, London, 1988.

Inland Revenue, *Property Market Report*, Autumn 1988.

Inspectorate of Pollution, First Annual Report, HMSO, 1989.

Jones, Maclean and Young, *Islington Crime Survey*, London, 1986.

*Labour Force Survey*, HMSO, bi-annual.

David Leigh, *The Wilson Plot*, London, 1989.

London Housing Unit, *Another Disastrous Year for London's Homeless*, 31.12.1987.

Low Pay Unit, *The Poor Decade*, London, 1988.

W.J. MacLennan, 'Subnutrition in the elderly', *British Medical Journal*, 293, 1986.

MAFF, *Household Food Consumption and Expenditure 1984*, Annual Report of the National Food Survey Committee, HMSO, 1986.

Manpower Services Commission, *Labour Market Quarterly Report*, September 1987.

MIND, *Report to Sir Roy Griffiths' Review of Community Care*, July 1987.

*Mortality Statistics*, HMSO, annual.

Alistair Mowat, 'Rheumatoid Arthritis', *The Practitioner*, July 1983.

MORI Poll, *Child Abuse*, September 1984.

MORI Poll, *Young People*, May 1988.

MSL, survey, *Discrimination Against The Over-40s*, London, 1989.

National Association of Victim Support Schemes, *Annual Report 1987-88*.

National Housing and Town Planning Council survey, *Gambling Machines and Young People*, 1988.

Nature Conservancy Council, *Nature Conservation in Great Britain*, 1984.

*New Earnings Survey*, HMSO, annual.

# SOURCES AND REFERENCES

OPCS, *Heights and Weights of Adults in Great Britain, 1980*, HMSO, 1984.

OPCS, *Occupational Mortality, 1979-80, 1982-3*, HMSO, 1986.

OPCS, *Occupational Mortality, Childhood Supplement*, HMSO, 1988.

David Piachaud, *Poor Children: A Tale of Two Decades*, Child Poverty Action Group, 1986.

Police Monitoring and Research Group, *Police Response to Domestic Violence*, London, 1986.

*Population Trends*, HMSO, quarterly.

John Posnett, 'Trends in the Income of Registered Charities, 1980-85', in *Charity Trends, 1986-87*, Charities Aid Foundation.

Prison Reform Trust, *Teenagers, Prisons and the Courts*, 1988.

*Prison Statistics, England and Wales*, HMSO, annual.

*Probation Statistics, England and Wales*, HMSO, annual.

Rape Counselling and Research Project, *Rape, Police and Forensic Procedure*, Submission to the Royal Commission on Criminal Procedure, 1979.

*Regional Trends*, HMSO, annual.

G. Rose and M.G. Marmot, 'Social class and coronary heart disease', *British Heart Journal*, 45: 13-19, 1981.

Royal College of Physicians, *Health or Smoking?*, 1983.

Saladin Security Systems, *White Collar Crime in the UK*, London, 1989.

Joni Seager and Ann Olson, *Women in the World*, London, 1986.

Shelter, *Christmas Report on Homelessness*, London, 1988.

Andre Singer, *Battle for the Planet*, London, 1987.

Peter Singer (ed.), *In Defence of Animals*, London, 1984.

Alwyn Smith and Bobbie Jacobson, (ed.) *The Nation's Health*, London, 1988.

*Social Security Statistics, London*, HMSO, annual.

*Social Trends, London*, HMSO, annual.

*Statistics of Experiments on Living Animals, Great Britain*, HMSO, annual.

Don W. Steele, 'Alcohol', *Long Range Planning*, Vol. 20, No. 5, pp. 86-90, 1987.

Swann Report, *Education for All: The Report of the Committee of Inquiry into the Education of Children from Ethnic Minority Groups*, HMSO, 1985.

Nina Taylor (ed.), *All In A Day's Work*, LER (Lesbian Employment Rights, 1986).

*That's Life!*, Survey On Tranquillisers, BBC, 1985.

Peter Townsend and Nick Davidson (ed.), *Inequalities In Health* (The Black Report), London, 1982.

*Transport Statistics, Great Britain*, HMSO, annual.

Alan Walker and Carol Walker, *The Growing Divide*, Child Poverty Action Group, 1987.

Water Authorities Association, *Water Facts*, London, annual.

Water Authorities Association, *Water Pollution From Farm Waste*, London, 1988.

Margaret Whitehead, *The Health Divide*, Harmondsworth, 1988.

WHO, *Targets for Health for All: Targets in Support of the European Regional Strategy for Health for All by the Year 2000*, Copenhagen, 1985.

J.K. Wing (ed.), *Schizophrenia: Towards a New Synthesis*, London, 1978.

# USEFUL ADDRESSES

## Part One: Health
Department of Health
— Social Security Statistics, Central Office, Newcastle-upon-Tyne NE98 1YX. 091-279-7373.
— Statistics of Personal Social Services and Health Services, Hannibal House, Elephant and Castle, London SE1 6TE. 01-703-6380.
Health Education Authority, Mabledon Place, London, WC1. 01-387-9528.
Office of Health Economics, 12 Whitehall Street, London, SW1. 01-930-9203.

### Abortion:
Birth Control Trust, 27 Mortimer Street, London W1. 01-580-9360.

### Suicides and Parasuicides:
Samaritans, 46 Marshall Street, London W1. 01-439-2224.

### Accidents:
RoSPA (Royal Society for the Prevention of Accidents), Cannon House, Priory Queensway, Birmingham. 021-200-2461.
Consumer Safety Unit, Department of Trade and Industry, Room 306, 10-18 Victoria Street, London SW1. 01-215-3215.
Department of Transport, 2 Marsham Street, London SW1. 01-276-3000.
Health and Safety Executive, Old Marylebone Road, London NW1. 01-229-3456.

### Diseases:
Cancer Research Campaign, 2 Carlton House Terrace, London SW1. 01-930-8972.
Institute of Neurology, 1 Wakefield Street, London WC1. 01-837-0113.

### Disabled:
Disability Alliance Educational and Research Association, 25 Denmark Street, London WC2. 01-240-0806.

### Blind:
Royal National Institute for the Blind, 224 Great Portland Street, London W1. 01-388-1266.

### Deaf:
Royal National Institute for the Deaf, 105 Gower Street, London WC1. 01-387-8033.

### Deaf-Blind:
SENSE, The National Deaf-Blind and Rubella Association, 311 Grays Inn Road, London WX1. 01-278-10 · 05.

### Cerebral Palsy:
Spastics Society, 12 Park Crescent, London W1. 01-636-5020.

### Mental Handicap:
MENCAP, 123 Golden Lane, London EC1. 01-253-9433.

### Down's Syndrome:
Down's Syndrome Association, 12-13 Clapham Common South Side, London SW4. 01-720-0008.

### Autism:
National Autistic Society, 276 Willesden Lane, London NW2. 01-451-3844.

### Epilepsy:
National Society for Epilepsy, Chalfont St. Peter, Bucks. 02407-3991.

# USEFUL ADDRESSES

**Arthritis:**
Arthritis and Rheumatism Council for Research, 41 Eagle Street, London WC1. 01-405-8575.
**Diabetes:**
British Diabetic Association, 10 Queen Anne Street, London W1. 01-323-1531.
**Back Pain:**
National Back Pain Association, 31 Park Road, Teddington, Middlesex. 01-977-5474.
**Heart Disease:**
British Heart Foundation, 102 Gloucester Place, London W1. 01-935-0185.
**Mental Illness:**
MIND, 22 Harley Street, London W1. 01-637-0741.
**Schizophrenia:**
National Schizophrenia Fellowship, 78 Victoria Road, Surbiton, Surrey. 01-930-3651.
**Affective Psychoses:**
Manic Depression Fellowship, c/o Richmond CVS, 51 Sheen Road, Richmond, Surrey. 01-332-1078.
**Smoking:**
ASH (Action on Smoking and Health), 5-11 Mortimer Street, London W1. 01-637-9843.
**Alcohol:**
Action on Alcohol Abuse, 11 Carteret Street, London SW1. 01-222-3454.
Alcohol Concern, 305 Grays Inn Road, London WC1. 01-833-3471.
**Solvent Abuse:**
Institute for the Study of Drug Dependence, 18 Hatton Place, Hatton Garden, London EC1. 01-430-1991.
**Television:**
Independent Broadcasting Authority, 70 Brompton Road, London SW3. 01-584-7011.
BBC Television, Television Centre, Wood Lane, London W12. 01-743-8000.

## Part Two: Welfare
**Poor:**
Child Poverty Action Group, 1 Bath Street, London EC1. 01-253-3406.
**Debt:**
Support in Debt, 1 Linksfield, Denton, Manchester.
**Unemployed:**
Unemployment Unit, 9 Poland Street, London W1. 01-434-9509
**Low Pay:**
Low Pay Unit, 9 Upper Berkeley Street, London W1. 01-262-7278.
**Pensioners:**
Help The Aged, St. James Walk, London EC1. 01-253-0253.
**Single Parents:**
National Council for One-Parent Families, 255 Kentish Town Road, London NW5. 01-267-1361.
**Children in Poverty:**
National Children's Home, 85 Highbury Park, London N5. 01-226-2033.

# USEFUL ADDRESSES

**Homeless:**
Shelter, 88 Old Street, London EC1. 01-253-0202.
**Poor Housing:**
Association of Metropolitan Authorities, 35 Great Smith Street, London SW1. 01-222-8100.
**Education:**
Department of Education and Science, Elizabeth House, York Road, London SE1. 01-934-9000.
Independent Schools Information Service, 56 Buckingham Gate, London SW1. 01-630-8793.
Adult Literacy Basic Skills Unit, 229 High Holborn, London WC1. 01-405-4017.

## Part Three: Relationships
**Adoptions:**
British Agencies for Adoption and Fostering, 11 Southwark Street, London SE1. 01-407-8800.

## Part Four: Freedom
**Sexual Discrimination:**
Equal Opportunities Commission, 1 Bedford Street, London WC2. 01-379-6323.
**Racial Discrimination:**
Commission for Racial Equality, Elliot House, 10-12 Arlington Street, London SW1. 01-828-7022.
**Anti-Gay Discrimination:**
LAGER (Lesbian and Gay Employment Rights), Room 203, South Bank House, Black Prince Road, London SE1. 01-587-1643.
**Civil Liberties:**
National Council for Civil Liberties, 21 Tabard Street, London SE1. 01-403-3888

## Part Five: Public Order
**Child Abuse:**
NSPCC (National Society for the Prevention of Cruelty to Children), 67 Saffron Hill, London EC1. 01-242-1626.
**Victims:**
National Association of Victim Support Schemes, 39 Brixton Road, London SW9. 01-735-9166.
**Prisoners:**
NACRO (National Association for the Care and Resettlement of Offenders), 169 Clapham Road, London SW9. 01-582-6500.

## Part Six: Environment
Department of the Environment, 2 Marsham Street, London SW1. 01-276-3000.
**Pollution:**
Friends of the Earth, 26-28 Underwood Street, London N1. 01-490-1555.

# UCEFUL ADDRESCES

**Toxic Waste:**
HM Inspectorate of Pollution, 3 East Grinstead House, London Road, East Grinstead, West Sussex. 0342-312016.

**Water Pollution:**
Water Authorities Association, 1 Queen Anne's Gate, London SW1. 01-222-8111.

**Sea Pollution:**
Marine Conservation Society, 4 Gloucester Road, Ross-on-Wye HR9 5BU. 0989-66017.

**Countryside:**
Council for the Protection of Rural England, 4 Hobart Place, London SW1. 01-235-9481.
Nature Conservancy Council, Northminster House, Peterborough, PE1 1UA. 0733 40345.
Royal Society for the Protection of Birds, The Lodge, Sandy, Bedfordshire. 0767-80551.

**Monuments and Buildings:**
English Heritage, 23 Savile Row, London WQ1. 01-734-6010.

**Animals:**
British Union for the Abolition of Vivisection, 16a Crane Grove, London N7. 01-700-4888.
RSPCA (Royal Society for the Prevention of Cruelty to Animals), Causeway, Horsham, West Sussex RH12 1HG. 0403-64181.
Ministry of Agriculture, Whitehall Place, London SW1. 01-270-8080.
League against Cruel Sports, 83-87 Union Street, London SE1. 01-407-0979.

## Charities:
Charities Aid Foundation, 18 Doughty Street, London WC1. 01-831-7798.

# ACKNOWEDGMENTS

The author and editors would like to thank the following for permission to use photographs:
Andes Press Agency 126; Barnaby's 117, 118; Camera Press 34, 105, 161, 171, 173; Colorific/Black Star/Lynn Johnson 41; William Cheung 156; Downs Syndrome Association 43; Friends of the Earth/Chris Rose 149; Sally and Richard Greenhill 54, 62, 69L, 88; Greenpeace/Dorreboom 160, Greenpeace/Hadley 146; Barry Greenwood 129; David Hosking 163TR; Eric Hosking 163BR; Eric and David Hosking 163TL; Impact/John Cole 33, Impact/Christopher Pillitz 58; Lawrence and Beavan 169; League Against Cruel Sports 172; Network: Mike Abrahams 60, 68R, 79, 98, Katalin Arkell 81, 115, John Cole 91, Chris Davies 107, Geoff Franklin 45, 50, 69R, Roger Hutchings 148, Barry Lewis 10, 38, 42, 63, 82, 152, Neil Libbert 72, Laurie Sparham 50, 53, 64, 76, 101, John Sturrock 13, 25, 75; News Team 150; The Observer/Ben Gibson 159; Photo Co-op: 131, Gina Glover 83, Crispin Hughes 68R, 84, Wayne Tippetts 85; Popperfoto 23, 86, 111; Press Association 108, 130; Rex 17, 18, 21, 22, 40, 122, 135; Samaritans 14; Science Photo Library/Dr Tony Brain 29, Science Photo Library/James Stevenson 46; Select: D. Martinez 155, Nick Owen 166, Mark Pinder 91R; Sion Touhig 56; ZEFA 97, 164, 167. Picture research by Charlotte Lippmann and Elizabeth Loving.

Illustrations by Jennie Smith.

# INDEX

# INDEX

# INDEX

# INDEX

# INDEX

suicides, 14, 15, 20, 71
sulphur dioxide, 147, 148-9
Supplementary Benefit, 70, 83
survival rates, cancer, 29
swimming accidents, 23

tax fraud, 130
teenagers: abortions, 12; homelessness, 83; parasuicide, 15
television, 62
terrorism, 118, 119, 122
theft, 126
toxic waste, 150-1, 160
trade unions, 108, 123
traffic jams, 167
trains, accidents, 17, 20-1
tranquillisers, 61
transport accidents, 16-23; air, 22; railways, 17, 20-1; road, 17, 18-19; at sea, 23
trials, legal rights, 118
tunnels, air pollution, 147

ulcers, peptic, 46
unemployment, 70, 72-3, 110
unemployment benefit, 74
universities, 89, 90

vacant land, 165
vandalism, 131
victims, crime, 140
violence: against the person, 132; child abuse, 137; domestic, 133; murder, 132, 134-5; racial, 132
vivisection, 168-9
voting system, 117

waste: nuclear, 152-3; toxic, 150-1, 160
water, drinking, 156
waterways, pollution, 154-5
wealth, inequality, 64-5
weapons, 127, 128, 129, 131
weight, overweight, 49

wheelchairs, 35
women: breast cancer, 29, 30; cervical cancer, 29, 31, 55; childcare, 109; domestic violence, 133; occupations, 106-7; in power, 108; sexual discrimination, 104-5
work *see* employment

All Optima books are available at your bookshop or newsagent, or can be ordered from the following address:

Optima, Cash Sales Department,
PO Box 11, Falmouth, Cornwall TR10 9EN

Please send cheque or postal order (no currency), and allow 60p for postage and packing for the first book, plus 25p for the second book and 15p for each additional book ordered up to a maximum charge of £1.90 in the UK.

Customers in Eire and BFPO please allow 60p for the first book, 25p for the second book plus 15p per copy for the next 7 books, thereafter 9p per book.

Overseas customers please allow £1.25 for postage and packing for the first book and 28p per copy for each additional book.

# MORE BOOKS FROM OPTIMA

*Friends of the Earth Handbook* edited by Jonathan Porritt, £4.99, ISBN 0 356 12560 2, printed on recycled paper.

'This handbook is compiled by staff and supporters of Friends of the Earth and contains all the practical advice you need to become a good environmentalist.' *The Guardian*

*Green Pages* compiled by John Button, £9.99, ISBN 0 356 14432 1, printed on recycled paper.

'Empowering, useful, witty and highly recommended. . . . This book considers the deeper questions of where our society is going, and how we can choose alternative directions in many aspects of our lives.' *She*

*Green Manifesto* Sandy Irvine and Alec Ponton, £6.99, ISBN 0 356 15200 6.

Selected as an *Observer* Top Twenty title for the 1989 Green Book Fair.
    'Do you sincerely want to be green? If so, buy this book.' *Books*

*Guide to Gaia* Michael Allaby, £6.99, ISBN 0 356 17535 9.

In this book, Michael Allaby outlines the evidence for the Gaian hypothesis, and shows how it can be used to look at environmental problems in a new way.
    'This is an important book.' *The Sunday Times*

*The Allotment Book* Rob Bullock and Gillie Gould, £4.95, ISBN 0 356 12890 3.

Recommended by BBC Radio 4's 'Gardeners' Question Time.'

*Down the Drain* Stuart Gordon, £5.99, ISBN 0 356 17944 3.

*Down the Drain* is a scathing indictment of how we abuse and misuse water — our most valuable natural resource. It investigates the whole range of issues related to water pollution and privatisation.

*The Future is Now* Deirdre Rhys-Thomas, £4.99, ISBN 0 356 17947 8.

'Nobody can be proud of the fact that the Irish Sea is a dustbin, and I think it's absolutely tragic that Britain has refused to stop the dumping of sewage sludge into the North Sea.' Stanley Clinton Davies

'The greatest danger to the planet Earth is the existence of the animal man.' Tom Conti

In these frank and illuminating interviews, Michael Aspel, Pamela Stephenson, David Puttnam, Emma Thompson, Clive Ponting, Tom Jones and Claire Rayner are among people from both sides of the Iron Curtain in the media, the arts, public affairs, science and health professions who voice their concerns about the environmental dangers facing our planet.

*CND Scrapbook* Joan Ruddock, £9.95, ISBN 0 356 14019 9.

'Telling and moving testimony to the lengths ordinary folk will go to to safeguard the future.' *Time Out*

This book traces the history of the Campaign for Nuclear Disarmament in photographs, newspaper headlines, badges, posters and leaflets.

*Drug Warning* David Stockley, £6.95, ISBN 0 356 12424 X.

Compiled by the Metropolitan Police, and based on their own in-service training pack, this book offers a completely factual guide to all the different drugs being misused.

*One Parent Plus* Jane Ward, £5.99, ISBN 0 356 15846 2.

Whether you are separated, widowed or chose to have a child alone, *One Parent Plus* gives you the information you need to survive as a single parent; benefits, the law, and organisations which can give you specialist help and advice.

*Stepfamilies Talking* Elizabeth Hodder, £4.99, ISBN 0 356 15642 7.

'In Britain alone, six million people are members of stepfamilies. And with each new family created by separation and divorce, there are problems. These are covered in *Stepfamilies Talking* by the founder of the National Stepfamily Association.' *Daily Mirror*

*Second Time Around* Elizabeth Martyn, £5.99, ISBN 0 356 17235 X.

*Second Time Around* draws upon numerous case histories and interviews with people from a variety of backgrounds, and pinpoints the many areas where the aftermath of a failed marriage creates difficulties for people trying to forge a new relationship.

*Break-Up* Dr Masud Hoghughi, £5.99, ISBN 0 356 15817 9.

Written by the presenter of the Yorkshire TV series *Why Couples Break Up*, this book is about understanding what happens between two people that brings about the end of an intimate relationship, and it aims to help reduce the confusion, guilt and suffering experienced by many.

*Back to Work* Gemma O'Connor, £5.99, ISBN 0 356 15197 2.

'A book that offers positive advice' (*Chat*) on all aspects of returning to work.

*Choices in Healthcare* Elaine Farrell, £5.99, ISBN 0 356 17137 X.

Whether you need to find a local G.P. or a private specialist, facilities for a home birth or hi-tech maternity care, negotiate the waiting lists or take out health insurance, evaluate long-term or respite care for a relative, this book will guide you around the choices. Such guidance will be increasingly important as the changing role of the health services places greater emphasis on customer choice.

*Your Cancer, Your Life* Dr Trish Reynolds, £6.95,
ISBN 0 356 15417 3.

'For advice on your rights and explanation of
treatments, *Your Cancer Your Life*
is recommended.' *Woman's Journal*

*Cervical Smear Test* Albert Singer FRCOG and
Dr Anne Szarewski, £5.99, ISBN 0 356 15065 8.

Recommended by the Family Planning
Association.
    'An excellent book which should allay
women's fears about cervical cancer testing . . .
*Cervical Smear Test* provides a comprehensive
and illustrated guide.'
*Daily Mirror*